Known Upon Earth

A Study Guide to the Old Testament

Uniform with this volume

Life Forever

A Study Guide to the New Testament

O God be gracious and bless us,
and let your face shed its light upon us.
So will your ways be known upon earth
and all nations know your saving help
Psalm 67

Known Upon Earth

A Study Guide to the Old Testament

Instruction, a reading guide, and activities
for schools, bible study groups and private use by

Sister Mary Lenaghan FDNSC

COLLINS

Collins Liturgical Publications
187 Piccadilly, London W1V 9DA

First published by the Catholic Press, Vunapope, Papua New Guinea, 1977
First published, this edition, 1980

ISBN 0 00 599641 4

Imprimatur:
Johannes Hoehne MSC, Archbishop of Rabaul, 1 December 1976

Made and printed in Great Britain
by William Collins Sons & Co Ltd, Glasgow
Typeset in Univers by
Westholme Graphics Ltd, Cambridgeshire

For my nieces and nephew —
Maggie, Gerda and Nick

Note to the student

There is no need to write your answers in this book. The lines and spaces have been put in just to help you to set out your answers in your own exercise book.

Contents

The Old Testament books were inscribed on scrolls like this one

UNIT ONE
Using your Bible

If you wish to read the Bible, the first thing to do is to get *a good modern translation*, for example:

GOOD NEWS BIBLE
THE JERUSALEM BIBLE (JB)
THE REVISED STANDARD VERSION (RSV)

Which translation of the Bible are you going to use in this course? ________

1. The Contents

The contents of the Bible are usually arranged under two headings:

THE OLD TESTAMENT
THE NEW TESTAMENT

(Perhaps there will be a section in the contents for maps, notes, etc).

a. Open your Bible at the *contents*. Complete;

The Old Testament goes from page ________ to page ________
The New Testament goes from page ________ to page ________
Are there any maps in your Bible? ________ How many? ________

- You can see from the contents that the Bible is really a collection of books; it is in fact, *a library* rather than a *book*.

b. Write down the full name of three Old Testament books. ________
Write down the full name of three New Testament books. ________
Find these books *in* the Bible itself.

- You often find the name of a book written in a short form, for example:

The Book of Genesis = Gen
The Book of Exodus = Ex

c. In most Bibles a list of short forms (or abbreviations) is given. See if this list is in your Bible and complete:

The Book of Deuteronomy = _________
The Book of Proverbs = _________
The Book of Jeremiah = _________

d. Spend a long time looking at the contents. Get used to:

i. The names of the books.
ii. Where they are in the Bible.
iii. Which are Old Testament and which are New Testament books.

2. Practice in looking up references

You will notice that each book is divided into *chapters* and *verses*.

a. Take for example the **Book of Genesis**.
How many chapters are there in this book? _________
How many verses in Chapter 1? _________

b. Write down the first verse in the Bible. (This verse is referred to as **Gen 1:1**).
Complete:

Gen 1:21 tells us that God made _________
Gen 6:13 tells us that God decided to _________

c. Read the following passages and choose the correct answer:
Ex 6:1 tells that:
God saved Noah.
God spoke to Moses.
Abraham offered a sacrifice to God.

Num 3:1 mentions:
Moses and Aaron.
Abraham and Sarah.
Cain and Abel.

Deut 8:7–10 describes:
A person.
A land.
A religious feast.

Prov 15:18 gives;
A commandment.
A wise saying.
A prayer.

d. Practice in finding references. See how quickly you can find:

Num 14:11; Dt 33:1; Ps 55; Is 3:16; Mic 7:14; Mt 11:28; Lk 17:6; Rom 5:6.

3. Jewish and Greek bibles

There were many religious books in Palestine before the birth of Jesus and many were written at the beginning of Christian times. The Jews at that time had to decide which, out of all these books, were **sacred** and should therefore be put into their Bible. They decided that, out of all of them, only *twenty-four* were **sacred** and they grouped these under three headings:

1. THE LAW
2. THE PROPHETS
3. THE WRITINGS

Modern Jews still use this Jewish (or Hebrew) Bible and many Christians have it as their Old Testament. (The Old Testament is about God's preparation for the coming of Jesus and His saving work.) In the 3rd century BC, there were many Jews living in Egypt in the city of Alexandria and a translation of the Jewish Bible into *Greek* was made for them. However, the people who prepared this Greek translation believed that some sacred books had been left out of the Jewish Bible and so they put these into the Greek Bible. Here they are:

Book of Tobit
Book of Judith
Book of Wisdom
Book of Ecclesiasticus
Book of Baruch
1 and 2 Maccabees

The first Christians used the Greek form of the Old Testament; they agreed that all the books in it were sacred books and this is why the Catholic Church kept the Greek form of the Old Testament and, in time, added the New Testament books to it.

a. Is the **Book of Ecclesiasticus** in the translation you are using? ________

Besides the number of books, there are other differences between the Jewish and the Greek Bibles; we will note only two of them:

i. In the Greek Bible the books are *grouped in a different way* from those in the Hebrew Bible; they go under these headings:

HISTORICAL BOOKS
WISDOM BOOKS
PROPHETICAL BOOKS

ii. *The Psalms* in the Hebrew Bible *are numbered differently* from those in the Greek Bible. (Good News Bible, The Jerusalem Bible and the Revised Standard Version follow the Hebrew numbering.)

n.b. In this Course, the Hebrew numbering is always given.

Special note
The Jewish people gave the LAW first place in their Bible; they said it was God's special gift to them. It taught them how to live in a way that was pleasing to God and how to worship Him. This was what all good Jews wanted to know. They liked to think of the LAW as one book with five sections in it namely: Genesis; Exodus; Leviticus; Numbers; Deuteronomy, and they always linked its contents with *Moses*. They often called the LAW by another name, the *Torah.* We call it the *Pentateuch,* a name that was made up from two Greek words meaning 'five scrolls'.

In ancient times, people often wrote on dried strips of animal skin or on sheets of copper, or on papyrus (made from part of a plant), and when they had finished, they rolled up their work. Rolled-up writings like these are called *scrolls*. Probably all the books of the Bible were done like this in the first place. (You will learn more about the LAW in Unit 4.)

- We Christians give the *Gospel*, which is the good news that we have been saved, first place in the Bible; we think of it as God's special gift to us and find in it the way to life forever with God.

b: Write down the opening sentence of the **Gospel according to St Mark** __________

4. Reading the Bible

Everyone needs someone to help him or her to read the Bible because it is different from an ordinary book. (Remember that some people say it is a library!) With an ordinary book, we usually begin at the first page and read right on to the end. If you tried to do this with the Bible, you would soon feel lost and disappointed. The way to read it for the first time is to read only certain passages and leave out others. Later when you go back and read the parts you left out, you find them very interesting and helpful.

In this Study Guide, the main passages to be read are always given in **bold type.**

5. The Bible is an eastern book

We know from experience that there are people with different languages, customs and cultures from ours and that it takes a long time to learn to understand and appreciate them. In the Bible we meet *Eastern People* who lived long ago in ancient times. Their names, customs, laws, activities, money, calendar, etc., are all *Eastern* and if we want to understand and appreciate these people, who are indeed most interesting, we have to work hard. Fortunately, there are many books besides the Bible itself that can help us with background study.

Background study to the Bible is so important because it helps us to get the right religious message from the sacred text.

a. If you get a chance, look in a library or bookshop and write down the names of two or three books that could help you to understand the people of the Bible lands.

b. Look at the Map I on p.25 of this Study Guide. Spend time getting used to the names of countries, rivers, seas, etc. (On a modern map of the Middle East, you would find new names and divisions.)

6. The Bible is God's Word

- Even though it is very important to know that the Bible is an eastern book from ancient times, there is something much more important. *The Bible is God's Word to all mankind.* Through the Bible, God tells us about Himself and His saving work and He invites us to live in a holy way so that we can have a good life on earth and be happy with Him forever in heaven.

  Reading God's Word and thinking deeply about it brings us joy; it helps us to know and love God more and gives us a strong desire to make "His ways known upon earth".

Let us begin our study of the Bible with this prayer:

"Teach me your ways, O Lord;
make them known to me.
Teach me to live according to your truth,
for you are my God, who saves me.
I always trust in you." Ps 25:4 – 6

UNIT TWO
What the people of Israel believed about the beginning of the world and mankind

In the first chapters of the Book of Genesis you can read what the people of Israel believed about the beginning of the world and of mankind.

In telling about their beliefs, the People of God made use of stories and ideas that also belonged to other near eastern people, but they used them in a way that showed *their own special beliefs.* There was nothing like these in all the religions of the ancient Near East. The reason for this is quite clear to us because we know that they were *revealed by God Himself.* This is the reason too, why they hold for people in every period of history and every level of culture. For many centuries, the people of Israel handed on their beliefs by word of mouth, but a time came when *different stories* containing them were written down. Perhaps about five hundred years before Jesus was born, these different stories were collected and grouped together and put at the beginning of the **Book of Genesis**, the first book of the Bible. It would be a mistake for us to think that these stories are exact descriptions of what happened or to think that the sacred writer is looking at things from the point of view of science or history. No. He is just telling us, in a very beautiful eastern way, what his people believed about the world and mankind.

Genesis 1:1 – 2:4a* is sometimes called the **first creation story**. In it the creation of the world is described as the Work of God, planned out and spread over six days. As you read it, you must admire the order and beauty of God's work which was all done for a purpose and without effort or help or bother from anyone. Notice especially that everything that comes from God is good; evil does not start in Him. This story is presented as a carefully planned poem. When you are reading it, try to think of a long pendulum swinging and you will enjoy reading it aloud in time with the even swing of the pendulum.

Read **Genesis 1:1 – 2:4a**

1. God in creation

a. Write down the words that tell us that God is first; that He was there before creation ________

This idea often comes up in the Bible. You will find it, for example, in **Is 48:12**.

* v.4a means the first half of verse 4; v.4b means the second half of verse 4.

b. Count how many times *God* is mentioned in **Gen 1:1 – 2:4a**. Complete;
The sacred writer has mentioned God ________ times. This makes us realize that God ________

c. Which verse tells us what it was like before God used His creative power? ________
Read it aloud. What happens when you try to imagine this scene? ________

Darkness: In the Bible darkness usually suggests confusion and evil. There is no darkness in God; He scatters darkness. In this creation story, God turns it into something by bringing it under His control.

d. Write down *the two words* that tell us that God *wanted to create* and that He did so without effort or help or trouble. ________ ________

God's Word: God's WORD has *in it* the power to do whatever He wants. Look up **Is 55:10 – 11** and **Ps 147:15 – 18**.

Days of Creation: You must have noticed already that God's work of creation is divided into days. There is no need to think that "day" means twenty-four hours, or that creation took one week. The divisions of God's work over the period of a week has a religious lesson for us. It reminds us that there is a time for working and a time for resting (that is the meaning of the Hebrew word "Sabbath") and it is pleasing to God to keep this day of rest in His honour.

- We Christians follow this teaching by keeping the Sunday holy and at the same time, we show our dependance on Christ, the only Saviour.

e. Look at **verses 4** and **5**. You will see that God did three things. Complete, and then read the comment;

i. He ________
Comment: Whatever God sees to be in line with His will is good. This is because He is all-Good.

ii. He ________
Comment: This introduces the idea of dividing. This is a most important idea, because it tells us that God gives each thing its own place in creation.

iii. He ________
Comment: The person who makes a thing is the one who has the right to give it a name. So from this creation story we learn that everything belongs to God.

f. One way to stress a point is to repeat it often. Notice how many times the sacred writer tells us that everything God made is good. Why do you think that this is such an important point? ________

g. As you read more of the Bible you will see that everything is under God's control. He

might use His power over creation *to reveal* Himself, or *to save*, or *to punish*. Look up these references:
Jer 10:12 - 14; Ex 17:1 - 7; Jer 14:1 - 10.

In which one does God reveal Himself? ________
In which one does God save? ________
In which one does God punish? ________

Divine activity: We could say that this *creation story* is full of *divine activity*. God does things like speaking, seeing, dividing, etc. Only a living, intelligent being can do these things and the people of Israel realized this. They loved to call God *the living God*. You can find this expression in many places in the Bible. Other peoples had gods of their own, but the religious leaders of Israel taught that these gods had no life and could do nothing.

h. Read **Is 44 and Ps 115**
Write the words that tell of God's respect for the Sabbath: ________

Note: In His time, Jesus noticed that many religious leaders of the Jews exaggerated the importance of the Sabbath; they made it more important than anything else in religion and He corrected them for this.

Look up **Mk 2:23 – 28**.

i. Use these words to complete this summary:
depends; control; before; creator; living; place; good; things.

The God of Israel is a ________ God. He is the ________ of all things. He gives each thing its own special ________ . He does not need ________ Himself. He was there ________ anything was made. Everything ________ on him and is under His ________ . He does only what is ________ .

j. In the book of Job there is a long passage about God the creator. Just as you have learnt about God from the work of creation, so did Job.

Read **Job 38 – 42:1 - 6**

k. In their prayers, the people of Israel liked to praise God for His work of creation. Turn to the **Book of Psalms** and read **Ps 104.** Try to memorize a few verses.

Write you own prayer or hymn praising God for creation.

2. Human beings in creation

Our study of human beings in creation begins with **Gen 1:26.** As you read this verse you will feel that God's creative activity is reaching a climax. God stops in His work and holds a mysterious discussion about the next "thing" that He intends to make.

a. Write out **verse 26.**

We must look very closely at this verse to try to discover what it tells us about human beings.

i.
"And now we will make ________ ".
From these words we can see that God has a *special interest* in human beings. Before, He used expressions like 'Let the earth produce'; now He says *'We will make'.*

ii. *"They will be like us and resemble us".*
In ancient times it was customary for a king to leave a statue (image) of himself in a country that belonged to him. So God acts like a near eastern king – He leaves an image of Himself in the world; His is a *living image* that can plan and act responsibly.

iii.*"They will have power ________ ".*
These words tell us that God wants human beings to plan and act.

b. Read each verse and the comment on it:

v.27: *"He created them male and female".*
Comment: This is how the Bible explains the origin of sex and society. Man and woman are equal in God's eyes and necessary to each other. Together they build up society.

v.28: *"He blessed them".*
Comment: From this blessing we know that it is God's will that human beings co-operate with Him in forming living images of Himself.

v.28: *"Have many children".*
Comment: Human beings are to live together with others.

v.29: *"I have provided".*
Comment: God wants human beings to have what is necessary for life.

c. Use these words to sum up what the Bible has told us so far about human beings:
plan and act; representatives; social; equal; will; society; place.

Human beings are God's ________ on earth. Like God, they can ________ responsibly. Man and woman are ________ in God's eyes. They are ________ beings and it is God's will that they should co-operate with Him in building up ________ . Like all other created things, human beings have their own special ________ in the world.

3. More about God and man

Note i: Some people like to call **Gen 2:4b-25** the **second creation story**. It is not a poem like the first account, but rather a delightful near eastern story. In it, you find that all God's attention is directed towards *man.*

Note ii: Clay was very important to the people of the ancient Near East. They used it for making bricks; they wrote on it and they made all kinds of things for household use from it. A person who works with clay is called a potter.

a. What would you expect of a good potter?
i. __________ ii. __________ iii. __________

Read **Gen 2:4b - 9**

Explanation: The sacred writer wants us to know that God gave loving attention and used all His skill in making man. So he tells us God is a potter who takes clay and moulds it carefully into the shape He wants. This done, He brings it to life with His own life. And so man has something *from the ground* (earthly) and something *directly from God* (heavenly). This is why he is different from all other creatures (they are from the ground only), and different from God who is *uncreated.*

The sacred writer wants us to know now that all creation is *for man* and so he says God is a gardener who lays out a fine garden for him. In this way, God gives man what he needs, makes him happy and allows him to develop himself.

- Very often the Bible speaks of God *as though He were* a human being. This is one important way it has of helping us to know God but *it never says that God is a human being.*

b. Read **Gen 2:4b - 9** again, thinking of the explanation given above.

Read to the end of **Chapter 2**.

c. Write out **verse 9b**.
Can you make a mental picture of this tree in the same way as you can an apple tree, banana tree, etc.?

d. Write the words that tell us that God wants to take responsibility __________

e. Which verses tell us that man must answer to God for what he does? __________

f. Which verses tell us that God put man in control of the animals and birds that He had made? __________

g. How do we know that man realized he was different from animals and birds? ______

Note: It was pointed out earlier that the sacred writer is not giving an exact description of what took place in the beginning. He wants his readers to pay attention to the *religious meaning* in what he writes, so that they will have a sure foundation for their relationship with God, with each other and with the world.

h. How does the Bible explain that man and woman are the *same kind* of being? ______

Marriage: In **verse 24** the Bible comments on marriage. We learn that:

i. Marriage is *of divine origin,* not human.
ii. In marriage there is a relationship that is *exclusive,* i.e., it shuts out all others.
iii. Marriage is *permanent.*

i. Write down the words in **verse 24** that tell us that the marriage relationship is exclusive and permanent __________ .
Jesus Himself quoted **Gen 2:24** when the Pharisees asked Him about divorce.
Read **Mk 10:1 - 10.**

j. The sacred writer concludes his comments on the creation of man by telling about the perfect relationship there was between man and woman.

Write down the words he uses: __________

Read **Psalm 8** that sings of the glory of God and the dignity of man; and, if the **Book of Ecclesiasticus** is in your Bible, read **Eccles 17:1 - 14,** which are the thoughts of a wise man of Israel on creation. *These references ought to be read in a prayerful way.*

Like the wise man of Israel we can be still sometimes, too, and think about the wonder of creation. Since we belong to Christian times we have *another and even greater creation* to think about. It is the **new creation** that came through Christ's sacrifice on Calvary. By faith in Christ, and baptism, we *share in this new creation.* St Paul saw that Christ is *first* in the new creation.

Read **Col 1:15 - 20.**

In every eucharistic celebration we are reminded of creation and of the new creation. The bread and wine remind us that creation is a gift from God and so in a spirit of joy and thanksgiving, with admiration for the creator, we place bread and wine on the altar. On behalf of the Church, the priest accepts our gifts of bread and wine and changes them into the Body and Blood of Christ. In this way food from the ground becomes food from heaven, the food of the new creation.

4. The disobedience of man

In a way it could be said *the theme* of **Genesis 1 – 2** is *the relation between God and Man,* and this theme is carried on in **Ch. 3.** The sacred writer judged that the best way for him to give his readers an understanding of how this relationship developed was to make use of a kind of religious story that was appreciated very much among his people.

It allowed him to give his explanation in symbolic language. As you read **Gen 3:1 – 13** you will see that man wanted to decide for himself what was good and what was bad and to do as he liked. His idea was 'to go up' into God's place; to stop being a creature of God and to become *the same* as God. And so it was that *the first sin was a sin of pride* – pride that showed itself in disobedience.

Read **Gen 3:1 - 13.**

Symbols: All people make use of *symbols.* Take for example, Christians. One important symbol they have is a cross. It 'speaks' to them; it says things like this:

– You have been redeemed.
– You must suffer.
– Through Christian suffering and death, you will come into glory.
– All the blessings you enjoy have come to you through the death of Christ on the cross.

When trouble or sorrow comes to a person we sometimes say, "He/She has a heavy cross to carry." When Our Lord told His followers to take up their cross daily and follow Him, He was using symbolic language.

a. Complete: A lighted candle is a Christian symbol for: ________
b. Name any other symbol you know. What does it 'say' to you? ________

You see now that a symbol is an easy way of putting great and deep thoughts into our minds.

In the Ancient Near East the *snake* was an important symbol. To some people it 'spoke' of good things like protection, new life and health; to others it 'spoke' of evil powers and disorder. The first time in the Bible that the snake is used as a symbol is in this very old story of the fall that you have just read and no one is quite sure what this symbol meant to the earliest people of Israel. Only much later on in their history, and gradually, did the people of Israel give this symbol a *special meaning of their own:* they made it stand for the devil or Satan. Perhaps in those very far-off times it made the woman think of something good like new life or freedom from death.

It would be good to read **Gen 3:1 - 13** again, keeping in mind what you have just learnt about symbols, because now you understand that the sacred writer is using symbolic language to explain that something very serious went wrong between God and man right back near the beginning; that man by rebelling against God, broke up the beautiful order God put into creation and into the heart of man and brought in evil instead.

c. Write down the words that tell us that man knew that something had gone wrong.

____

The loving-kindness (mercy) of God towards sinners is seen for the first time in **verse 8.** God Himself went looking for the man and the woman; He did not leave them alone with their dreadful feelings of guilt and shame; He did not break off relations with them altogether.

Gen 3:15 is sometimes called the *first Good News.* Here, in loving kindness, God is promising that a time will come when evil will be conquered. He is giving human beings a *hope to live by.*

d. **Gen 3:21** tells us that God made Adam and Eve feel at ease in His Presence. He did not leave them without grace; He made peace with them.

How does the sacred writer explain this? __________

e. How do we know that the way of life God had intended for Adam and Eve and their children was finished forever? __________

f. How do we know that blaming others for the things we do does not hold with God?
____

- As you go on with your study of the Bible, you will realize more and more that it was only because of God's *loving-kindness* that we were saved. The New Testament people saw this clearly.

Read **1 Pet 1:3 - 4**

Very often at Mass we hear this prayer:

"Father, in love you created man,
in justice you condemned him,
but in mercy you redeemed him,
through Jesus Christ Our Lord."

We should often think about the fall and the punishment, because all of our problems are connected with these, and they are the background to God's saving work.

The New Testament explains fully the passage about the fall.

Read **Rom 5:12 - 20**

On Good Friday the liturgy sums it up like this:

"By a tree we were enslaved,
and by the cross we are set free.
The fruit of a tree was our undoing;
the Son of God has redeemed us."

5. The sin stories

We know from the big punishment God gave Adam and Eve that their sin was very great in His eyes. The three sin stories that follow help us to realize even more how serious this first rebellion against God was. It opened the way to every kind of sin; sin that spread all through the human race destroying the good relationship God intended man to have with Himself; with other human beings, and with all creation.

A. CAIN AND ABEL: Gen 4:1 - 15

a. In this story, which verses:
   i. describe the sin? __________
   ii. give the punishment? __________
   iii. tell of reconciliation? (reconciliation = making friends again) __________

b. After you have thought about this story yourself, turn to **1 Jn 3:12** and write down St John's thoughts about Cain. __________

Turn to **Heb 11:4** and write down the author's thoughts about Abel. __________

B. THE FLOOD STORY: Gen 6:5 – 9:17

When you read the Flood Story, remember *that this is a story about* **sin.** In it, sin is like an ugly disease spread all through society. It is something so disgusting in God's eyes that He uses His divine power to wipe it out. God can distinguish between good people and sinners; He can save and punish. His loving-kindness can be seen in the fresh start He allows the human race to have.

There are many flood stories from ancient times besides this one in the Bible. Floods are common disasters, and they are always a good subject for stories. The flood story "The Epic of Gilgemesh", that came from the people of Babylon, is the one most like Noah's flood, but even so, people find these two stories quite different in religious content.

As you read the flood story you will notice that some details are repeated and that others are difficult (impossible!) to work out, e.g., what did Noah take into the Ark? People who have studied this story closely know that different accounts of the flood story were handed down among the people of Israel. The sacred writer wove these together in a way that interested him (remember he was a near eastern man) and allowed him to give his message in a clear way. This sort of thing happens a lot in the Bible and it is not so difficult to understand when we realize that stories and pieces of information were handed down orally in different parts of Palestine for hundreds of years and recorded by different people. The person (or group) who finally gathered them together was very careful to see that nothing important was left out.

Many scholars have a great interest in finding how each book of the Bible was put together, and they can tell us a great deal, but all the same, we must never forget that God Himself watched over the formation of the scriptures and wanted us to have them just as they are now.

Turn back to the second paragraph at the beginning of this unit, p.13, and read it again.

c. Read **Gen 6:5 – 9:17.**

Which verses tell:
   i. about the sin? __________
   ii. about the punishment? __________
   iii. about the reconciliation? __________

d. After you have thought about this story yourself, turn to **Lk 17:20 - 30** to see the lesson that Jesus drew from this old story that had been handed down among His people.

Write down what the lesson was: ________

e. Turn to **Heb 11:7.** Why did the author praise Noah? ________

- Following the thought of St Peter in **1 Pet 3:20-22,** the early Church saw in the flood a clear *symbol* of baptism. In baptism guilt is washed away and we are given a fresh start, a new life in God.

C. THE TOWER OF BABEL STORY: Gen 11:1 - 9

In this sin story the sacred writer makes use of an old story about a famous tower in Babylon. The Babylonians used to build a special type of tower that went up by stages. It is called a ziggurat and usually it was built beside a temple. People are not sure what it symbolized. Some think that it stood for the earth; others say that it was a sort of divine mountain that was supposed to be a link between heaven and earth.

As you read **Gen 11:1-9** remember this is a story about *sin.* Some people make the mistake of thinking it is a story about the beginning of language!

f. Read **Gen 11:1-9**

Which verses describe:
i. the sin? ________
ii. the punishment? ________

g. You might have noticed that the other sin stories followed this pattern: *sin, punishment, reconciliation.*

In what way is this one incomplete? ________.

- At the Last Supper Jesus prayed for *unity* and by His death He conquered sin which scatters and divides. (See **Jn 17:20-26** and **Jn 11:51b-52**).

The Spirit of the risen Jesus brings *unity* to all races and nations. At Pentecost, the *unity* that was lost at Babel was restored 'for each man heard the apostles speaking in his own language'. The *reconciliation* necessary to complete the pattern in the Babel story took place at Pentecost when God's loving-kindness towards sinners was fully revealed.

In the last book of the Bible you can read St John's wonderful vision of the *unity* we will experience when Christ comes at the end of time.

Read **Rev 7:9-17.**

When time is finished, then there will be 'the new heaven and the new earth', that is, the new creation and the work of God begun 'in the beginning' will be complete.

Between the first creation and the new creation lies the **history of salvation** *described in the Bible, in which we all share through faith in Christ.*

UNIT THREE
Famous ancestors of Israel

It is clear from the sin stories that fallen man was under the power of sin; it could attract him, rule his life and destroy him altogether. God saw this and in His loving-kindness planned out the **work of salvation** which spread over nearly two thousand years. God began this work at a definite *time* in history and at a definite *place,* HARAN (you can find it on Map I), and with a particular person, ABRAM. Right from the start, God made the success of His plan depend on man's willingness to co-operate with Him. In this way, He restored man's dignity and gave him a way of life fitting for a Son of God.

Salvation history begins at **Gen 12:1.** If you like, you can think of this as the beginning of the work of the new creation. You will notice that it begins in the same way as the work of creation, with God speaking: 'God said'. From **Chapter 12** on to the end of Genesis the sacred writer describes the history of the famous ancestors of the people of Israel (usually called the *Patriarchs*). In doing this he used a form of story called the *saga* OR *legend.* This form of story was very popular with the people of the Bible. It allowed them to reach far back into their past, to make it sound splendid and to find some message there. The saga style also allowed the writer quite a lot of freedom. He did not have to put historic events in their proper order and he could exaggerate here and there to help make his point clear. In Unit Two you learnt about a form of story that allowed the writer to give his religious message in symbolic language. Later on you will have examples of other forms of writing. *It is always most important to know what form of writing is being used because this helps towards getting the right meaning out of a passage.*

Like the stories in **Gen 1–11,** these patriarchal stories were handed down orally for a very long time before they were fixed in writing as they are now. The main character is Abraham, a homeless man from Mesopotamia who lived about 1,800 years before Jesus was born. God *'called'* him and promised him countless descendants and the fertile land of Canaan.

People who study ancient times say that the patriarchal sagas give a very good picture of the lives of men and women of the Near East of that period, namely early 2nd millennium. The manners and customs referred to in the sagas are quite true of those times. This has been proved from many discoveries, but most especially from a big collection of writings (on clay) from *Nuzu.* These are dated about 1,500BC. Once a very old drawing was found on a tomb in Egypt; it shows a group of Semites (Abraham's race) visiting Egypt. The men have beards and the women have long hair held in place by bands. They have brightly coloured clothes; the men are wearing short skirts and sandals and the women have long dresses fastened at the shoulder. From this drawing, dated about 1,900BC, we can get a fair idea of how Abraham and his family must have looked. This kind of information which is so interesting helps us to

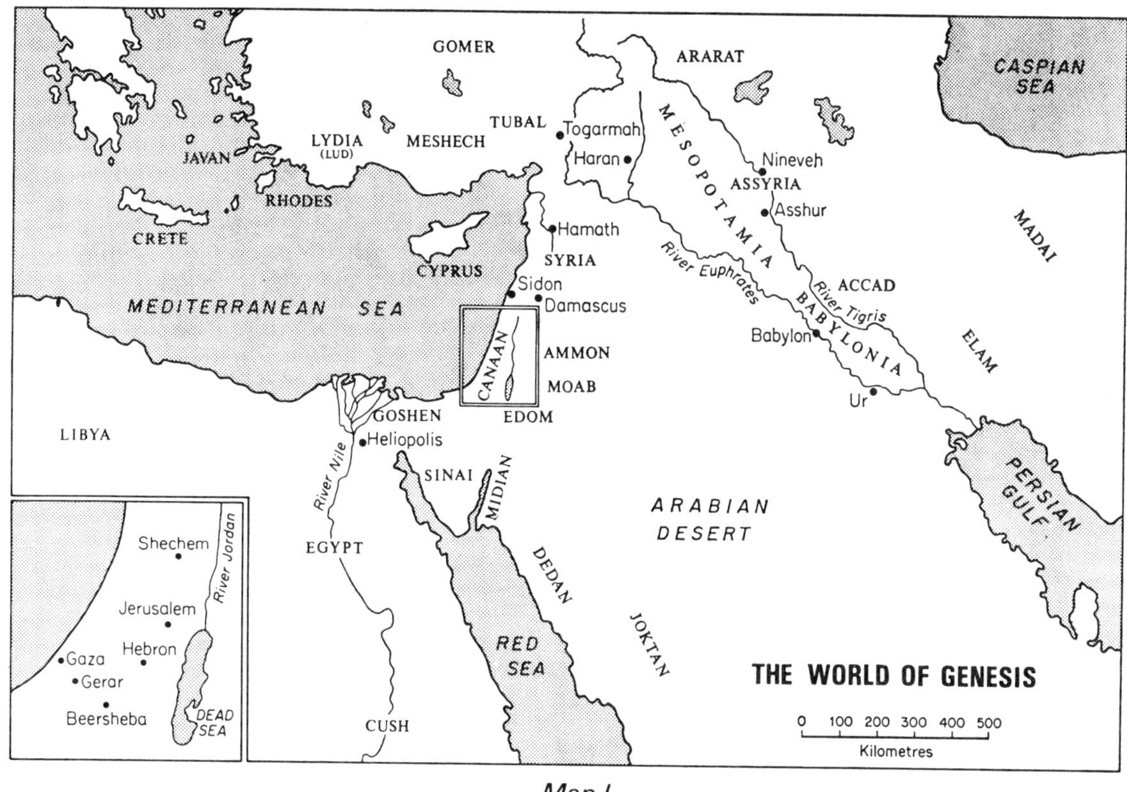

Map I

realize that the people of the Bible were real people, and that God accepted them with all their manners and customs.

As you read the lively stories of the patriarchs you are sure to wonder about the bad behaviour in the lives of these great people. Remember, they did not have Jesus as their model and His wonderful teaching to live by; they were at the beginning. Even so, they co-operated with God in **faith** and so His *saving action* is quite clear in their lives. We can admire the way He accepts them *as they are* and takes His time in educating them and leading them to higher moral values. And indeed it is the same with ourselves. As long as we try to co-operate with God in faith, His saving action goes on all the time in our lives. He loves us *now as we are,* patiently instructs us in His ways and gradually sanctifies us through His Word and sacraments.

- From these stories of the Patriarchs, we learn what is valuable in God's eyes and as we read them, His grace comes to help us to value these same things ourselves.

1. GOD'S CALL TO ABRAM

Read **Gen 12:1-10**

a. Write down God's *promise* to Abram. __________

b. Write down something you have learnt about God from **Gen 12:1-10.** ________

c. Look up **Rom 4:3.** What was it that made Abram pleasing to God? ________

2. ABRAM AND LOT SEPARATE

Read **Gen 13**

a. How did Abram show generosity towards Lot and trust in God? ________

b. Which verses tell us that God renewed the *promise* to Abram? ________

3. ABRAM RESCUES LOT

Gen 14 describes a battle that took place between nine kings in the valley where Lot had settled. He was captured and taken off as a prisoner.

Read **Gen 14:17-24**

a. Who honoured Abram? ________

b. How did Abram show that he trusted God completely? ________

c. Which verse makes us think of the Eucharist? ________

Salem is Jerusalem and it means 'peace'. It is an honour for Abram to be linked with Jerusalem, which was God's Holy City. Melchisedek is a figure of Jesus who is both king and priest. In Jerusalem, in front of the Roman governor, Jesus said He was a king and in that city, as the great High Priest, *made peace* between God and man through His sacrifice. With the thought of Jesus' sacrifice in his mind, St John describes another holy city which he calls the New Jerusalem. This is the heavenly city of the *new creation,* shining with the glory of God and it is the home of all those who have been saved.

Read **Rev 21:9 – 22:5.**

4. GOD'S COVENANT WITH ABRAM

Even though a long time had passed and now Sarah was too old to have a child, Abram still held *in faith* to the *promise* God had made. Chapters 15 and 17 are different stories of how God renewed His *promise* and entered into a special bond (called a *covenant bond* or *covenant relationship*) with Abram.

Note on **covenant:** In ancient times covenants (that is, agreements or contracts) were often made and concluded with a ceremony rather like the one described in **Gen 15:9-17.** This was a way of making the people realize that contracts are serious things. People who made contracts like this had special obligations to each other; in a way, they became like brothers and sisters. The agreement in **Ch 15** is one-sided. Only God passed between the divided animals; He bound Himself to the *promise;* but in **Ch 17** it is two-sided.

Read **Gen 15 and 17**

a. What does the name Abraham mean? _________

b. What does the name Sarah mean? _________

c. What did Abraham have to agree to? _________

Note 1: Names are very important in the Bible. They might describe a person's character or appearance, recall an important event, tell about a person's vocation. Very often when someone was called to a special work, *his name was changed to suit his new calling.*

Note 2: Circumcision is a small operation in which the foreskin is removed from the penis. This was a common practice among many near eastern peoples. They did it for different reasons, but the people of Israel did it for a religious reason. For them, it was *the mark or sign that they belonged to God's chosen people.*

As a member of God's Chosen People, Our Lord Jesus Christ carried this mark. (See **Lk 2:21**.) In the early Church, in the time of the apostles, there was very much discussion about circumcision. Some thought that all those who wanted to follow Christ ought to be circumcised. St Paul was against this; he realized that it is the gift of the Holy Spirit that makes one a follower of Christ and a member of God's holy people. The whole matter was finally settled at a meeting of the Apostles in Jerusalem. You can read about this in **Acts 15:1-33,** if you like.

- For us, *baptism* is the mark or sign that we are members of God's holy people. In baptism we receive the gift of the Holy Spirit, and so we can take our place with all God's people around His altar to worship Him and to receive the bread of life. This is why baptism is so important to us. (God's holy people means the people He set apart for Himself.)

5. HAGAR AND ISHMAEL

To our way of thinking there is quite a lot of bad behaviour in **Gen 16.** Sarah grew tired of waiting for God to act on His *promise* and so she used a custom of the time to obtain a child. Ishmael was a child of nature, planned by Sarah – not the child of *promise,* and so the *promise* made to Abraham did not pass on to him.

Read **Gen 16.** Complete:

a. Abraham behaved badly by _________

b. Sarah behaved badly by _________

c. Hagar behaved badly by _________

6. VISITORS TO ABRAHAM

The *promise* to Abraham is put before us again in **Ch 18** and at the same time we are taught "nothing is too hard for the Lord".

Read **Gen 18:1-15**

Write a prayer to God, telling Him that you trust Him. Try to include the words "nothing is too hard for the Lord".

7. ABRAHAM PLEADS FOR SODOM

Read **Gen 18:16-33**

This is the first time the Bible speaks about the power good people have with God. You will come across many other examples as you read the Bible, e.g., **Num 14:11-20,** but the greatest examples are in the New Testament part of the Bible.

a. Read **Num 14:11-20**

b. Turn to **Lk 23:24** and write out Jesus' prayer for the people who put Him to death.

c. You might like to write one or two verses from the long prayer Jesus said for His apostles and for us. It is **Ch 17** of St John's Gospel.

d. Write a prayer asking God to have mercy on people who live in a sinful way.

8. THE DESTRUCTION OF SODOM AND GOMORRAH

Read **Gen 19:23-29**

a. Why did God destroy these cities? __________

b. Why did God save Lot? __________

c. *Read* **Lk 17:31-33**

- Lot's wife did not have her whole mind on the salvation God was offering her and so she died along with the wicked.
  In baptism, we are called out of the darkness of sin and offered eternal life in the Kingdom of God. We must have our whole mind set on eternal life. Jesus warns us against "looking back".

9. THE BIRTH OF ISAAC

Read **Gen 21:1-8**

a. The sacred writer gives several details that make us realize that Isaac was *the child of promise.* Write down two of them. __________

b. What happened to Ishmael, the child of nature? __________

10. THE SACRIFICE OF ISAAC

God had to teach the people of Israel that He did not want them to offer Him human sacrifices and that is perhaps the main reason why the Bible tells the story of the sacrifice of Isaac. They could offer Him animals, blood, corn, oil, wine, etc., but not human life.

Even though other people offered human sacrifices (like the king of Moab, **2 Kings 3:26-27,** God's people were not to copy them. As you can see from **Jer 7:31-34** some did, and a terrible punishment came on them.

Read **2 Kings 3:26-27** and **Jer 7:31-34**.

- Abraham's great love for God stands out clearly in the story of the sacrifice of Isaac; it makes us think of God's love for us. The child Isaac reminds us of Jesus carrying His cross to Calvary, the place of sacrifice.

Read **Gen 22:1-19**

a. What reason did the Lord give for blessing Abraham? In your answer use his exact words. __________

b. Write out **Jn 3:16** and learn it by heart.

11. ISAAC'S MARRIAGE

Before he died, Abraham sent his servant back to the land of Mesopotamia to his own relations to get a wife for Isaac. He did this because he was thinking of God and the *promise.* If Isaac were to marry a Canaanite girl, he might follow her gods and in the end fail to co-operate with his God.

It comes out very strongly in the Bible that God's people were not to marry foreigners who followed 'other gods'. Of course, many of them did, like Solomon and the men of Esra's time. **1 Kings 11:1-3** and **Esra 10:1-17** are two interesting passages about this matter.

- The Church carries on the teaching of the Bible about marriage and, thinking about our salvation, strongly advises us to marry someone who shares our own faith in God.

Read **Gen 24**.

a. Why did Abraham refuse to let Isaac go back to Mesopotamia? __________

b. How did God show His interest in this important family affair? __________

12. THE DEATH OF ABRAHAM

The death of Abraham is told in only a few verses. He was buried at Hebron beside his wife, Sarah, in the cave at Machpela, which he had bought from Ephron who belonged to a people called the Hittites. (You can read about Abraham's deal with Ephron in **Gen 23**.) Many years were still to pass before God would give the whole land of Canaan to Abraham's descendants, but at least Abraham was buried in the promised Land in his own piece of ground.

Read **Gen 25:7-10**.

Ecclesiasticus 44:19b-23 is a beautiful summary of Abraham's life. (Is this book in your Bible?)

In the Letter to the Hebrews, there is a long passage praising the great faith of Abraham. You might like to read it: **Heb 11:8-19.**

13. THE BIRTH OF ESAU AND JACOB

The sacred writer moves on rather quickly now to the next generation, to Esau and Jacob, the twin sons of Isaac. He does this because his attention is on the *promise;* he wants us to see what became of it and also he wants to prepare us for something very great in God's plan of salvation, namely *God's choice of the people of Israel.*

Perhaps you have already asked yourself, "Why did God choose Abraham? Why did He choose Isaac and not Ishmael?" This same question, or rather mystery, comes up stronger than ever with His choice of **Jacob** and, since it was Jacob's sons who were the ancestors of the twelve tribes of Israel, *God's choice of the whole people of Israel is seen in advance in His choice of Jacob.*

- The mystery of God's free choice of the *nation* or the *person* He wants appears over and over in the Bible. (Sometimes it is called the mystery of *divine election.*) When the nation, or person, *responds in faith,* God's saving work always goes ahead. We experience this same mystery among ourselves today and when the whole *Church,* or person, responds to God *in faith,* people are saved and made holy.

Read **Gen 25:19-34** and **Gen 27.**

Write a prayer to God thanking Him for choosing you in baptism and giving you the gift of eternal life.

14. JACOB

Jacob is the main character in the remaining chapters of Genesis. There are many stories about him and his remarkable son, Joseph, who saved the whole family by providing food during a long famine.

One of the most important stories about Jacob is told in **Gen 28:10-22.** Here, in a symbolic way, we are told that God means to have a special relationship with Jacob and his descendants. Sacred "business" will pass "up and down" between them.

a. Read **Gen 28: 10-22.** Write down Jacob's response to God. __________

b. It is wonderful to see God's saving plan unfolding in the life of this great Patriarch. Here are some stories about him for you to read: **Gen 29:1-30; 31:1-21; Ch 32; Ch 33; 35:1-21.**

c. In **Ch 32** we see that God changed Jacob's name. Write down the reason God gave for doing this. __________

Perhaps you are disappointed that there is not more in the Book of Genesis about Isaac, the child of *promise.* The sacred writer does not really overlook him because he makes the Jacob stories part of the "family history of Isaac", and he is careful to tell us that God renewed the Promise to Isaac (**Gen 26:24**).

In considering the sacred history of his people, the writer of the **Book of Ecclesiasticus** mentions Isaac and Jacob together. If this book is in your Bible read **Eccles 44:22-26.**

15. JOSEPH

Before reading the Joseph stories, go back and read **Gen 15:13-16;** this passage prepares us for what is to come and teaches us that people's lives are in God's hands. Joseph realized this and summed it up very beautifully in **Gen 45:5.**

a. Write out **Gen 45:5** and learn it off by heart.

b. Write a prayer asking God to watch over you and help you to do His will.

The Joseph stories continue the history of Israel's famous ancestors, and, while bringing it to a close, prepare for the next stage of salvation history, which centres on *God's choice* (or election) *of the people of Israel.*

Here are some stories for you to read: **Gen 37; 39; 41; 42:1-24; 45.**

c. Write down four good things in Joseph's character. ________

d. Write a short prayer asking God to help you to grow in one of these good things that you admire in Joseph. ________

16. EGYPT

The king of Egypt invited Joseph's father, his brothers and their families to come and settle in Egypt. He gave them land and, in time, they became rich and had many children. But Israel's great ancestors never lost their desire for the promised land.

Read **Gen 46:1-8; 46:28-34; 47:27-31; 49:29 – 50:26.**

a. Why did Jacob want his body to be taken back to Canaan? ________

b. Write out the verse that explains why Joseph did not want his body to remain in Egypt. ________

c. To find out what became of the *promise* read **Gen 49:8-10.** Complete:
The *promise* God made to the Patriarchs passed on to ________

Israel's great King David came from the tribe of Judah and so did Jesus Our Lord and Saviour. In the **Book of Revelation** He is called the "Lion of the Tribe of Judah".

d. Write out **Rev 5:5.**

With the death of Joseph a long silence seems to settle on the people of the Bible, but deep down in the heart of these ancient people the strong hope of their great ancestors was taking root.

- One of the most remarkable things about the great people of Israel *was the way they could wait in hope.* Sometimes it is good and helpful for us Christians to think of ourselves as *"a people who wait",* and to pray often, "Come, Lord Jesus".

  e. Write out **Jn 14:28a.**

  f. Read **Rev 22:6-21.**
  In every eucharistic celebration we express our faith in the coming of Jesus. We say:

  "Christ has died,
  Christ is risen,
  Christ will come again".

  g. Learn this prayer.

  Deliver us, Lord, from every evil
  and grant us peace in our day.
  In your mercy keep us free from sin
  and protect us from all anxiety
  as we wait in joyful hope
  for the coming of our Saviour, Jesus Christ.

UNIT FOUR
My people: your God

Right at the start, the sacred writer connects the people in the **Book of Exodus** with the Patriarchs. The patriarchs are their direct ancestors. With God's permission, they went down to Egypt and there, for a long time, enjoyed many blessings. They were well off and had many children. In Egypt they were called the *Hebrews.* We usually call them the *people of Israel* or the *chosen people.* Later on they were known as the *Jews.*

Perhaps five hundred years have gone by since God first spoke to Abraham and said, "Leave your country, your family and your father's house, for the land I will show you. I will make you a great nation."

As you read **Ex 1,** take notice of how much the *writer stresses the great increase in the people of Israel.* He wants us to realize that God is already carrying out part of His *promise* to Abraham. Quietly, in a quiet natural way, through the birth of children, He has been building up "the great nation". When the time comes for this nation to have its promised land, God will give it to them with a great display of power.

- When the divine plan of salvation is complete, we see the *promise* to Abraham in full light. Through Our Lord Jesus Christ, Abraham's descendants are all those who have been saved and the promised land is Heaven itself.

1. In Egypt

Read **Ex Ch 1.**

a. Write down two things that were done to stop the Israelites from increasing. ______

b. Who put an end to the Hebrew's good time in Egypt? __________

The "New King": Many people who study the ancient history of Egypt think that the "new king" was Seti 1 who ruled Egypt early in 13th Century BC. Ramases II came after him and treated the Hebrews in the same bad way. It is thought that they escaped during his reign. Both these rulers had big building programmes.

c. Write down the names of the cities that were built with Hebrew slave-labour. ______

The **Book of Exodus** that tells about the people of Israel leaving Egypt (Exodus = leaving or departure) contains *historical facts and it is on these historical facts that the religion of Israel* *stands.* In writing about them, the sacred writer used a form of writing called *religious epic:* he told the long story of the great events that happened at the beginning of the nation's history in a kind of poetic way. This form of writing made it easy for him to bring out the greatness of God and of the things He did out of love for the people He hoped would be His own.

- **Here is something you must realize**: *the people of the Bible always look at history from a religious point of view.*

REVISION: *Forms of Writing*

In Unit 2 you learned about **symbolic** writing.
In Unit 3 you learned about **sagas** or **legends.**
In Unit 4 you learned about **religious epic.**

Why is it important to know what form of writing has been used? (See Unit 3 p.24). __________

2. God remembers

In **Ex 2** the writer introduces MOSES as an extraordinary person whom God was watching over from birth; he is preparing us for the next important step in salvation history.

Read **Ex 2** and take special notice of **v.23-25.**

a. What did God remember when He heard the cries of the people of Israel? __________

Note: When God remembers, *He always does something.* Jesus who is God acts in the same way:

Read **Lk 23:42.** Write out this beautiful prayer, learn it, and say it often.

In our prayers, we say:
Lord, *remember* your Church. . .
Lord *remember* our brothers and sisters. . .

Read **Ex 3:1-20.** It tells us what God did:

b. Complete using one word: God __________ Moses

c. What was Moses told to say to the people of Israel? __________

d. What was he told to say to the king of Egypt? __________

The Divine Name: You must be wondering about the divine name given in **Ex 3:13-15.** This is really a mystery and a puzzle. One explanation that many scholars like is this:

God meant to keep His divine name a secret because in ancient times some people believed that once they knew the name of a god, they had power over that god.

Perhaps this explanation is not completely right, but it seems to be a good one, because the Bible always insists that God is the One who controls everything. You can see this, for example, in **Is 40:12-17** and **Rom 11:33-36.**

Ex 4; 5; 6:28 – 7:13 make it clear that *it was God who called Moses.* Moses did not set himself up as leader of the people. No. It was God who gave him this position. These chapters also make it clear that God acted freely out of love and pity for these descendants of the great patriarchs, and that He is *remembering* the *promise* He made first to Abraham.

It would be good to read all of **Ex 4, 5,** etc., but be sure to read **Ex 6:1-13.**

3. The disasters in Egypt

When you are thinking about the story of the disasters (plagues) in Egypt, remind yourself that it is written in the form of a religious epic, not in the form of a news report, or in some other form. Its purpose is to make known this truth about God:

God is Master of nature; He is Master of all races, no matter how powerful they may be: He is Master of history.

You learnt before that different stories, telling what the people of Israel believed about the beginning of the world and man, were passed on orally for a very long time, before they were finally gathered together and fixed in the way we have them now. It was the same with the patriarchal legends and with the disasters and, indeeed, with much that we read in the scriptures. When scholars look closely at the Bible text, they are often able to pick out the various traditions from the words used, or from the way of saying things, and sometimes they can trace the traditions back to their sources. This is very interesting and important, and perhaps some day you will be ready for study like this.

We often hear today about disasters like earthquakes, floods, diseases, or plagues of insects that destroy food, etc. People give all kinds of reasons why these things happen. When the sacred writer thought about the disasters in Egypt, he realized that nature is under God's control and that the disasters fitted into His saving plan for the people of Israel. Passing from disaster to disaster, the writer builds up the truth about God's power and prepares us for the greatest event in the Old Testament, namely, the EXODUS. In the Exodus, alone, without advice or help from anyone and with shocking suddenness, God destroyed the power and might of all Egypt.

Instead of reading the account of the disasters in **Ex 7:14f***, you might like to turn to **Ps 105,** which sums up all you have been learning about the sacred History of Israel.

Read **Ps 105**

a. Make a list of the disasters in **Ps 105** and then using the headings in your Bible, make another list from **Ex 7:14f.** What do you notice? ________

* **f** = following. So **14f** means v.14 and the following verses.

The king of Egypt was indeed a very hard person to deal with. Time after time, he took no notice of God's warnings and punishments and one more terrible disaster was necessary, the death of the first-born, before he would give in and let the people of Israel leave.

Read **Ex 11:1-10**

b. Which verse makes it clear that God deliberately favoured the Israelites? ________

4. Israel's Passover Festival

Long before the Exodus, the Israelites, like other people of the ancient Near East, kept feasts. For example, every year they had a festival in the springtime. In one part of it there was a ceremony that was intended to bring a blessing on their flocks. Blood was important in this ceremony; it was taken and rubbed on their tent-poles to frighten off evil powers. Another festival of theirs was the Feast of Unleavened Bread. This was held each year to celebrate the barley harvest. (There is really very much to learn about Israel's feasts and if ever you get a chance to do so, be sure not to miss it!)

From the time of the Exodus onwards, it seems as though these two feasts were combined into a single feast called the PASSOVER. It was still kept in the springtime, *but now its purpose was to celebrate the deliverance of the people of Israel from slavery in Egypt.* There were strict regulations about the feast.

Read **Ex 12:1-14**

a. Do you remember this sentence in Unit 3 – "When the nation or person responds in *faith,* God's saving work always goes ahead"? Write down two simple things the people had to do as part of their response in faith. ________

Note: Year by year, all over the world, Jewish people still celebrate the Passover. It is a family feast. For them, it is not just a time when they think about something that happened long ago when God passed over the homes of their ancestors in Egypt. No. When they celebrate it, *they undergo the same experience of deliverance as their ancestors.* The father tells his family: "This is the night God brought our *fathers and us* out of Egypt." During the celebration they love to remember that they are God's chosen people and to look forward to the complete and final deliverance that will be theirs when that great person whom they call the Messiah comes. (You will learn more about the Messiah later on.)

Why is it important for us to think about the Passover and about God bringing the people out of Egypt? This is the reason:

- The situation of the people of Israel in Egypt and God's saving work there resembles our situation after the fall of our first parents and the saving work of Jesus in bringing us out of the slavery of sin. Israel was saved by the blood of the lamb; we are saved by the Blood of Christ who is the true Lamb who takes away the sin of the world.

  You have just learnt how the very old Israelite feasts of blessing and harvest took on a new and deeper meaning after the Exodus, and how they were probably combined into the Passover Feast. Jesus always celebrated the Passover, but after the Last Supper this wonderful feast took on still a different and deeper meaning and its new name is the *eucharistic celebration* or *Mass.* Mass is not just a time when we think about the things that happened long ago during our Lord's last days on earth. No. *Every time we celebrate the Eucharist we experience, in faith, the saving mysteries of Jesus.*

The New Testament often speaks about Jesus as the true Paschal Lamb.

b. Look up **1 Pet 1:18-20** and **Jn 1:29.**

Ex 12:29-42 is an account of the night the people of Israel set out from Egypt. Take careful note of **vs 37,38.**

Read **Ex 12:29-42**

c. Who was in the group of people that left Egypt on the night of the Passover? ______

d. Look up **Ex 13:19** to see what happened about the *promise* the people had made long ago to Joseph.

The presence of God: From the time the people leave Egypt to start on their long and hard journey to the promised land, you will notice that there is a strong emphasis on *the presence of God.* He is always with His people in a special way. From being in His presence, they gradually learn to rely on His power, to respect His holiness, to rejoice in His company and to go to Him for advice. Later on, through their own fault, they had the terrible experience and sadness of being separated from Him.

Read **Ex 13:20-22.**

The Bible often contrasts the joy of being in God's Presence with the distress and suffering of being separated from Him. You find this especially in the **Psalms** which are so important and beautiful because they bring us into the prayer-life of God's people. It would be good if you could learn a few verses from the psalms off by heart, for example, **Ps 63:1-8** or **Ps 27:4-5** or **Ps 84:10-12** or take time to read one or two slowly, perhaps **Ps 42** and **Ps 77.** All these psalms express a longing for God.

- Like the Israelites, we are on a journey. Our journey should take us through this world into the promised land of heaven. As we go along we should try to grow in an awareness that God is with us and get into the habit of living in His presence. This is a sure way to happiness and peace and holy living.

5. The Crossing of the Red Sea

For the people of Israel, the crossing of the Red Sea was the most wonderful thing in all their

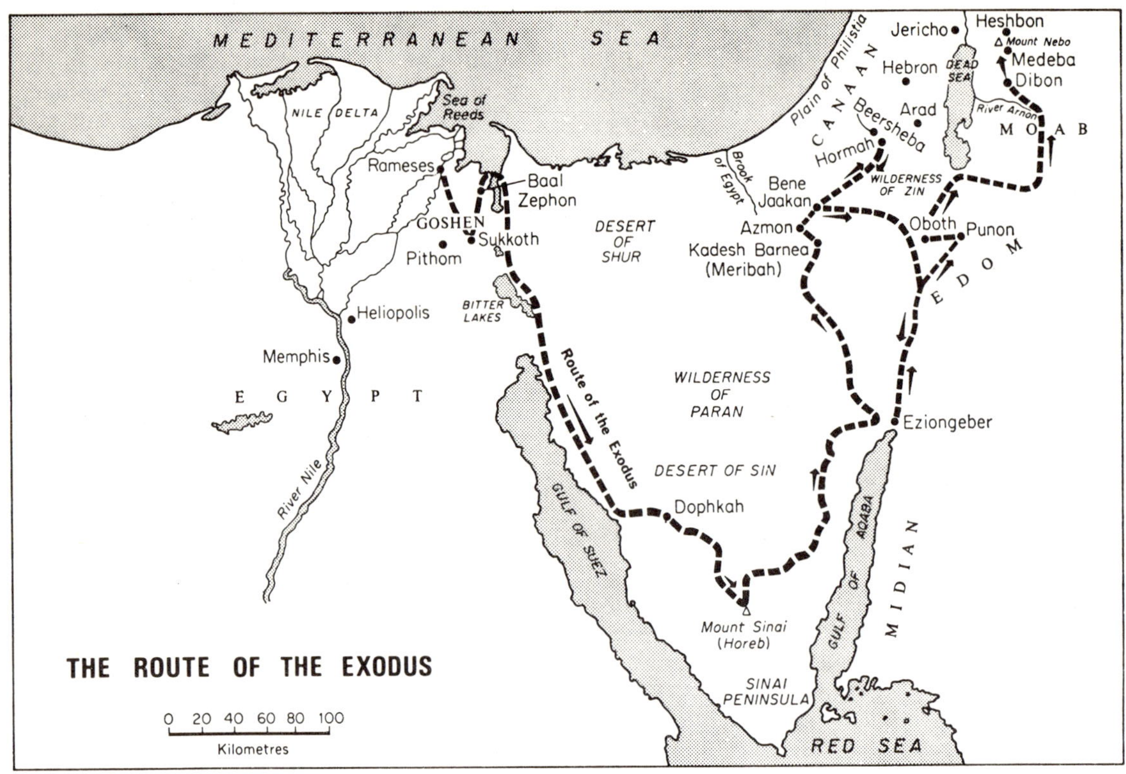

Map II

religious history. They saw it as a sure proof of God's power and of His special care for them, and of divine election (*Divine election* = chosen and called by God). It is most exciting to read **Ex 14** and the thanksgiving songs of Moses and Miriam in **Ex 15.**

There they were, these people chosen by God, trapped between the Red Sea and the great army of Egypt, powerless to save themselves. They fully expected to be wiped out of existence. Yet all they had to do was keep quiet and leave everything to God. As you read about God's saving action at the Red Sea, remember that it is written in epic form. Of course this does not weaken its religious meaning or lessen the wonder of God's power in any way. The sacred writer understands that God acted directly and powerfully for the sake of the people He specially loved. At the Red Sea, He was carrying out His *promise* to Abraham.

Read **Ex 14 – 15:1-21.**

a. Write down exactly what Moses said to quieten the people ________

b. You will find many references in both the Old and the New Testaments to the crossing of the Red Sea. Here are two that you could look up:
Ps 114 is full of wonder and praise;
1 Cor 10:1-6 is a strong warning based on a deep appreciation of God's power and holiness.

- Now what about us; have we crossed the Red Sea? The Church says, yes we have! It looks on the crossing of the Red Sea as a symbol of baptism. The waters of baptism separate us from the power of Satan and the slavery of sin:

> "Through the waters of the Red Sea
> you led Israel out of slavery,
> to be an image of God's holy people
> set free from sin by baptism".
> *(Easter Vigil: Blessing of Water).*

6. The journey to Sinai

The journey to Sinai is covered in **Ex 15:22 – 17:16,** but before reading this passage, stop and study Map II, *The Route of the Exodus.* This map shows the probable route of the Exodus. No one knows the exact route that the people followed, but some of the places they stopped at are known for sure.

Faced with the hardships of the desert, the people forgot about God's special love and power to save. Their faith was so weak that they soon fell into an ugly complaining attitude; they spared neither God Himself not their great leader, Moses. As you read **Ex 15:22 – 17:16,** you will be surprised at how often and how strongly they complained.

Read **Ex 15:22 – 17:16**

a. How did God show His patient kindness and saving power at: Marah ________
Elim ________
In the Desert of Sin ________

b. Besides complaining openly, how did some people show lack of trust in God? ____

c. How were the people taught reverence for the Sabbath? ________

It is interesting to read the accounts of God's saving work in the **Book of Numbers.** They are drawn from different traditions and have something to add to our faith and knowledge of God.

d. Read **Num 20:1-13; 11:4-16.**

Manna in the Desert: The full meaning of the "manna" in the desert becomes clear in the New Testament. After Jesus fed the five thousand men, He explained about the bread of life and, in instituting the Eucharist, He gave us the true bread from heaven, which is the food of everlasting life.

e. Read **Jn 6:25-59** and **Lk 22:17-21.**

f. Write out **Jn 6:54.** Learn this verse by heart.

7. At Sinai

In a conversation with Moses on Mt Sinai, God made known His desire to have a special bond or relationship with the people of Israel. He began by going over how He had shown His love for them in bringing them out of Egypt and then went on to say how He wanted them to *worship* Him and to be a *holy people.* He would leave them quite free to decide whether they wanted to come into this special relationship with Him or not. He made it clear that there would be obligations on both sides. He and they would have to have an exclusive and permanent love for each other, as in marriage. God would look after Israel always *if* Israel would obey Him.

From here on, we will call this special bond or relationship by its right name . . . . **covenant relationship.**

Revise the meaning of **covenant** (Unit 3 p.26)

Read **Ex 19:1-11a**

a. Who did God say He was? ________

b. What did He say He had done for the people? Use the words given in the text. ______

c. What privilege was He offering the people? ________

d. What responsibility would they have to take on IF they accepted this privilege? ____

e. Write the answer the people sent back to the Lord. ________

Once the *covenant* was made (or sealed) with the proper ceremony, *it could never be unmade.* God is faithful and unchanging; He does not say "yes" and then change it "no".

As we go on now with our study of salvation history, our *special interest will be in how the covenant relationship worked out and, from this, we should grow in the knowledge and love of God and learn to see ourselves in the People of Israel.*

On God's side, there is always *faithful love* and *kindness* and on Israel's side much *unfaithfulness* and *hard-heartedness.* God shows His faithful love and kindness in countless ways, e.g. by patience, by forgiveness, by renewing the covenant, by raising up good leaders, by making promises, by punishing etc., and lastly by sending His own Son among the covenant people to be their Saviour. In fact, God's whole loving plan was building up all the time to the complete and final salvation of Israel, and not only of Israel, but of the entire human race, in the new covenant which was sealed by the Blood of Christ. St Peter's instruction to the early Church helps us to appreciate the privilege of sharing in this new covenant.

f. Write down **1 Pet 2:9-11.**

The covenant people showed their unfaithfulness and hard-heartedness in many ways, e.g., by going after other gods, trusting them and worshipping them, by injustice, by greed, by pride in not listening to the leaders God sent them, by disobedience, by pretending to be good etc.

g. Read **Jer 7:5-12.**

Adultery and prostitution: The Bible often calls the unfaithfulness of Israel adultery and prostitution because it always remembers the exclusive and permanent relationship that was made between God and Israel at Mt Sinai.

h. Read **Hos 2:2-14.** (Baal = a god of the Canaanite People.)

8. A way of life

At Mt Sinai, God set out a way of life for the covenant people. This way of life would enable them to carry out their side of the covenant; it would bind them together as a holy nation and be the means of drawing all nations to the God of Israel. From the example of Israel they were to see the holiness and wisdom of God and want to be His People, also. It was Israel's vocation to be *the Light of the Nations.*

a. Write out **Is 49:6.**

- In the world today, it is the Church, the people of the new covenant, who are called to be the Light of the World. By the holiness of their lives, they are to draw all people to the praise and worship of God.

b. Look up **Mt 5:14-17.**

c. Write a prayer thanking God for the gift of baptism and asking Him to help you to carry out your Christian vocation.

The way of life that God wanted for His covenant people is summed up in the ten commandments (or Decalogue which means "ten words").

Read the whole of **Ex 20.**

d. If you do not already know the ten commandments, take time to learn them by heart.

Note: The ten commandments are written in a *form of legal writing* that was used in the Ancient Near East. It is very important to remember this. For one thing, it proves that the commandments were set down very early in Israel's religious history. It also helps us to accept them as they are and to go "behind" the form to discover the will of God in its fullness.

Since these *ten basic laws* had to be expressed in the daily lives of the people, they soon started wondering what they ought to do in different situations. To satisfy them, regulations had to be made about all kinds of things concerning daily life. The oldest of these regulations go back to the time of Moses and they were suited to the desert life. Later, when the Israelites became a settled people, new regulations were added and some of the older ones fell into disuse.

At last, after a very long period of time, many of Israel's regulations were gathered together and now we find them scattered through the Books of **Exodus, Leviticus, Numbers** and **Deuteronomy.**

Many of these regulations sound strange to us, *but behind each one of them there is a sacred purpose,* and that is why they were all so dear to the holy people of the Bible. Taken together with the commandments, they made up THE LAW. All those who were faithful to the covenant loved God's Law. They praised and thanked Him for it; they prayed for understanding of it and for fidelity to it. It was their life and their salvation. From **Ps 119** you can see the love and reverence there was in Israel for God's Law.

> Read **Ps 119.** This is a very long psalm, and you might be satisfied to read only part of it: **vs.97-105.**

True enough, there were many religious leaders in Israel who explained *the Law* to the people in such a way as to destroy its sacredness and turn it into a burden. This was still going on in Our Lord's time and He spoke out very strongly against leaders who were doing this. He was especially upset because people were being given a wrong idea of His Father. Jesus "explained" God so perfectly that He could say, "My yoke is easy and my burden is light", **Mt 28:30.**

9. The covenant is concluded

Remember that once the covenant was concluded, it could never be unmade. It was God Himself who suggested the covenant and Israel entered it freely.

The ceremonies that you read about in **Ex 24:1-18** mark the formal setting up of an exclusive and permanent relationship between God and Israel.

Read **Ex 24:1-18**

a. What did Moses say as he sprinkled the people with the blood of animals? Write his words as given in the test. ________

b. How did God and the leaders of Israel show that they were united and at peace? ____

c. In order to compare the concluding of the new covenant with the concluding of the Old, read **Lk 22:17-21.**
Write out **v.20.** ________

10. Worship

Not only were the covenant people to be *a holy nation,* they were to be *a people dedicated to the worship of God.* Immediately after the covenant is sealed, the sacred writer introduces things concerned with worship . . . namely, God's sanctuary and the priesthood.

Read **Ex 25:10-22** which contains instructions for making the Ark.

The Ark: The Ark was a kind of shrine that could be carried about (the Israelites were still a wandering people) and it was a symbol of *God's personal presence.* It was the place where people went to make peace with God and to communicate with Him. The Ark was carried ahead of the people as they made their way through the desert and when they went into battle they took it with them. Really, it was a constant reminder of divine election and of the covenant.

It will be interesting in Unit 6 to see what happened to the Ark in the end.

a. Read **Num 10:33-36.**

b. There are some references in the New Testament to the Ark. Read **Heb 9:4.**

Ex 28 is a chapter that contains instruction on priestly vestments. (You need not read all of this chapter, but just enough to make you realize how important everything connected with divine worship was.)

Read **Ex 28.**

The third Book of the Bible, **Leviticus,** takes up the matter of divine worship in a very detailed way. As a matter of fact, there are so many strange regulations in this Book that it is very difficult one to read. In the Books of **Numbers, Leviticus** and **Deuteronomy** you will find many more regulations about worship showing how important it was to the *covenant people.*

Read **Lev 1:1-17,** as a 'sample' passage to illustrate this point.

- Down through history, the Church has always tried to *preserve the sacredness of worship.* This is the reason why there are clear guidelines for the celebration of the eucharist and the sacraments. From the covenant people, we can learn to have a reverent approach to divine worship and a deep respect for the guidelines given us by the Church.

In all the great events of the exodus and covenant, it is remarkable that God always dealt with the people *through Moses.* We say the Moses was the **mediator** between God and the people. It was not God's way to deal directly with the people and this is how it was to be throughout salvation history. He always used a mediator and the greatest mediator of all was His divine Son, Jesus. On Calvary, it was through Jesus that a new and perfect covenant was made between God and man.

God's way of saving His people through a mediator is deeply rooted in the Bible and in the Church, who does everything *through Jesus Christ our Lord.*

The priests of the Church continue the work of Jesus, and so now God deals with us through them. He receives our offering at their hands and through them, gives us the Bread of Life, forgives us our sins, and instructs us in His ways.

Read **Ps 100** in praise of God for this wonderful way He has of dealing with us.

The Exodus: the People of God left the fertile land of Egypt, where they had worked as slaves to build the pyramids; they wandered for forty years in the desert with their flocks

UNIT FIVE
A nation and a land

The **Book of Numbers** takes up the story of Israel's journey from Mt Sinai (or Horeb) to the borders of Canaan. Mind you, it is not possible to work out from the text the exact road of the desert wanderings or even to put the events in the right order. This is not to say that the Book of Numbers does not contain real facts of history. Under God's guidance, the sacred writer selected certain facts and fitted them together in such a way that he was able to give his readers the religious meaning of Israel's desert experiences.

1. God and Israel

The **Book of Numbers** presents Israel as a people gathered together around God. He is always with His people, living among them, exercising His kingship and insisting on the covenant way of life. In this way He forms the mixed group of people who crossed the Red Sea (Ex 12:27-38) into a **nation**. It was God's presence and the way of life that He gave, that were the binding forces within this nation. True enough, God had good reasons for leaving it altogether, but His faithful love and kindness prevented Him from doing this. We have already remarked on the ugly complaining attitude this people had towards God and towards Moses. More than that, as soon as they met with a difficulty, they immediately lost faith in God, as though He had not proved His love and His power beyond doubt in the great events of the exodus!

But there was something even more offensive to God, and that was **apostasy** or turning to other gods. This was Israel's greatest sin against the covenant. This sin, committed in the desert so soon after the concluding of the covenant, was committed over and over again in the course of Israel's religious history, and when you come to study the Prophets, you will see the terrible consequences of it. Time and time again God's chosen people left Him and went off and worshipped other gods. In the light of the covenant relationship, it was like adultery.

Read the following references; they will help you to understand better what has just been said:

a. *God was always with His people:*
Num 9:15-23; Num 10:33-36
Complete: From reading these references I have learnt that God ________

b. *The people had an ugly complaining attitude:*
Num 11:4-7; Num 20:1-7.
Complete: From reading these references I have learnt that God ________

c. The people lost faith easily:
Num 13; 14. (We will look more closely at these Chapters in section 2, below.)

d. The people committed sins of Apostasy:
Ex 32:1-15. (Committed soon after the sealing of the Covenant.) **Num 25:1-6.**
Complete: From reading these references I have learnt that God ________

2. Israel's first attempt to enter Canaan

While the people of Israel were camped at Kadesh (see Map II, p.38). Moses chose twelve men and sent them into Canaan to get information about the land the people there. This was all in preparation for an invasion of the promised land.

Read **Num 13; 14.**

a. What did the men say about the land? ________

b. What did they say about the people? ________

c. Who occupied:
- i. The Negab? ________
- ii. The Highlands? ________
- iii. The coast and the Jordan Valley? ________

d. Who was in favour of going in and occupying the land of Canaan and why did they think it was possible to do so? ________

e. Who was against the occupation of the land and what did the people of Israel make up their minds to do? ________

f. Why did God regard the people's attitude as an insult? ________

g. Write out **Num 14:18.** ________

h. Why did God forgive the people? ________

i. What punishment did God give to those who rebelled against Him at Kadesh? ____

j. How did God reward Joshua and Caleb? ________

k. Why did the Israelites lose the battle against the Amalekites? ________

Joshua: Joshua means "God is salvation". The name "Jesus" is the New Testament form of Joshua.

Numbers: The Bible uses numbers in two ways:

- i. In an arithmetical way . . . like we do when we count, add, etc.
- ii. In a symbolic way . . . as when it gives a *special meaning* to a number.

Sometimes it is hard to decide which way a number has been used. People often say that 3, 4, 7, 10, 12, 40 and 70 are Biblical numbers, and they realize that they do not always know what they stand for. The study of Biblical numbers is a very special study and an important one because it opens up the meaning of Bible passages.

Read **Mt 18:21-23** where numbers are used in a symbolic way.

3. Israel's second attempt to enter Canaan

After a period of about one generation (forty years), it was decided to make another effort to enter Canaan. This time Moses planned to go through Edom, Moab and Ammon and to cross over the Jordan just north of the Dead Sea.

a. Look at the Map II, *Route of the Exodus,* p.38. (There was a road called the King's Highway that was used by traders and soldiers. It ran from Ezion-geber on the Gulf of Aqaba north through Edom and Moab. Probably Moses hoped to make use of this road and, since the Edomites were descendants of Esau, he expected that they would help the Israelites on their way.)

b. Read **Num 20:14-20; Num 21:1 – 22:1.**

The Israelites had *three* victories:

i. At Arad they defeated __________
ii. At Jahaz they defeated __________
iii. At Edrei they defeated __________

4. In the land of Moab

The Plains of Moab were the last stopping place of the Israelites outside the promised land. God is still present among them directing them *through Moses* and saving them from enemies.

In preparation for the invasion of the promised land and later, for the division of the land, Moses counted the people just as he did at Sinai, at the outset of the journey. He also gave very strong instructions that were intended to save the people from the religious practices of Canaanites.

Read **Num 26:63-65; Num 33:50-56.**

Up to now, we have been thinking of Moses mainly as the one *through whom* God dealt with the people of Israel, but he was also a great religious teacher. It would be a pity not to know something about the marvellous religious instructions he gave. These can be found in the **Book of Deuteronomy** and, even though this Book was not written until many years after the death of Moses, his instructions were well remembered in Israel. The sacred writer gives them to us here in the form of *sermons* given in the land of Moab.

Read **Deut 10:12-22; Deut 12:29-32; Deut 18:9-13.**

Note: **The Book of Deuteuronomy** Even though there is a very strong emphasis on *Law* in the Book of Deuteuronomy, it is still a very beautiful book to read. It stirs up in us a great love for God and a deep respect for His holiness, and it shows us that we have an excellent way of expressing our love for God, namely by keeping His commandments. Above all, it insists on the *great commandment,* and in this way teaches us that *love* is the foundation of religion.

5. End of desert wanderings

To conclude this phase of salvation history, turn to the song of Moses **Deut 32,** which sums up Israel's religious history in a lovely poetic way.

Read **Deut 32:1-44.**

Moses' work is over now and the time has come to find someone to take his place as leader and mediator.

Read **Num 27:12-23; Deut 34.**

a. Why did Moses ask God to appoint a new leader in his place? ________

b. Whom did God appoint? ________

c. What was the sign that Moses' authority was being handed on? ________

d. Did God intend to deal directly with Joshua as He had done with Moses? ________

e. Find Mt Nebo on Map II.

f. Who buried Moses? ________

g. Why was Moses called the greatest of the Prophets? ________

h. Write out the *great commandment,* **Deut. 6:5.** ________

At last Israel's desert wanderings are at an end and according to the divine plan, the time has come for God to give His people the land He promised Abraham. The desert years were to become a beautiful memory and to be seen as one of the most important periods in all Israel's religious history. There in the desert, the covenant people seemed to have God all to themselves. Day after day, for forty years, they *experienced* His divine presence, His faithful love and His saving power. Truly He was *their* God and they were *His people.*

6. Conquest and settlement

The Bible has kept two very different traditions of the conquest and settling down in Canaan, the promised land. From the **Book of Joshua,** you might get the idea that the conquest was achieved by one great effort of all the tribes united under Joshua; that it was sudden, fierce and complete. From the **Book of Judges,** it would seem that it was a long drawn-out process spread over two hundred years and never really complete. As you read passages from the **Book of Joshua,** try to realize that the writer is turning history into an *epic* to help his readers to realize how faithful God is to His promises. Through an entirely different presentation of history, the Book of Judges underlines this same truth.

A very important note: **The Holy War.**
You already know about some wars in which the people of Israel took part and there are many more accounts of wars like these in this part of the Bible that deals with the conquest and settlement in Canaan. Most of these sound very savage and cruel to us and probably you will be shocked and puzzled at what you read. But here is something you must understand: in the ancient world, people had the idea that war and religion were linked together and so in their eyes, war was a *holy thing; every war was a holy war.* It started at the command of a god (or goddess) and was carried on with his or her help. If victory was gained, then it was the god's victory and a proof of his power or his love for his people. God's people shared these thoughts about war and so the wars of Israel were looked on as God's wars and the enemies of Israel as His enemies. They thought of God as a warrior and a commander and they fought under Him. Remember how they always carried the Ark of God into battle! Whenever they won a battle, it was because God was with them.

There were very strict rules for the men going to battle; they had to be 'made holy' by certain practices. Whatever they won during the battle belonged to God; no one could keep anything for himself. The rule was that everything had to be destroyed. Whenever this rule was broken, God punished the offenders. When the sacred writer tells about the size of an army or how many people were killed, he could be *using numbers in a symbolic way* (not in an arithmetical way) to let us know that God's power to save or to punish cannot be measured.

7. Invitation to cross into the promised land

Read **Jos 1:1-10.**

a. How did God help Joshua to respond *in faith* to His invitation to go into the promised land? __________

b. Complete: Joshua would always be successful if __________

8. Crossing the Jordan

Read **Jos 3.**

a. How did the priests carrying the *Ark of the Lord* show their faith in God? ________

b. How did the people know that God was leading them across the Jordan? ________

c. Make a list of the people already living in the promised land? ________

Note: This list is not complete; there were others there besides these, for example, the **Philistines** who were to cause the Israelites quite a lot of worry in the years ahead. All these peoples had their own gods and religious practices and now God's people are going to have to live side by side with them. Remembering that they turned to 'other gods' even in the desert, what danger do you foresee?

9. The Capture of Jericho

The capture of Jericho which is told in **Jos 6** sounds more like a religious ceremony than a battle. Almighty God was at the head of the army directing the attack. Israel's enemies knew this very well and realized that they were not as strong as He was. Indeed, the whole city seemed to fall down from the strain and fear of having such a powerful God against it.

Read **Jos 6**.

a. How do we know that God was leading the Israelite army? ________

b. Why did everything in Jericho have to be destroyed? ________

c. Which biblical number occurs several times in this passage? ________

The rest of the Book of Joshua tells about three other victories – one in the centre, one in the south and one in the north of Canaan – and about the division of the land between the different tribes of Israel. If you would like to understand the holy war idea better, you could read **Jos 8:1-30; Jos 9; Jos 10:6-16.**

Map III, *The Division of Canaan,* shows you where the different tribes settled. If you would like to know more about the division of the land, read **Jos 14.**

10. The Shechem Covenant

At the end of his life, Joshua gathered all the people around him at Shechem and there acted as the mediator of a covenant. Joshua's covenant reminds us very much of the Sinai covenant and it follows *the same form.* First, the people hear God's title: **"The Lord, the God of Israel"**. Then they are told what He has done for them in the past so they can judge what to expect from Him in the future. Next, they are told what their duties will be and warned about not living up to them. Up to this point, they are quite free to enter into the covenant or not. The *mediator* waits for their decision. If they say "yes", he will set up a record or a memorial of the covenant.

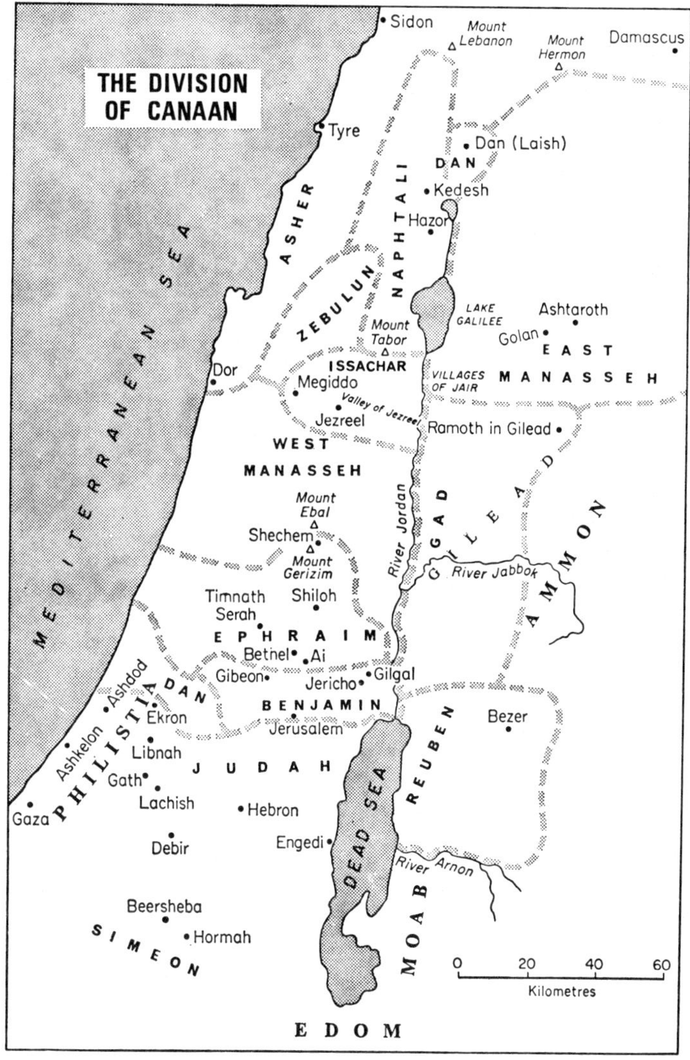

Map III

Read **Jos 24:1-28.**

a. In which verse do you find *God's title?* _________

b. Which verses give the summary of *what God has already done* for Israel? _______

c. Look at **verses 14, 25.** What *duties* would the people have? _________

d. Using the words of the text, write down the *people's decision.* _________

e. In which verse do you find the *record or memorial?* _________

Note: Other peoples besides the Israelites made agreements *in this same form.* We know this because records of ancient Hittite agreements have been found in Palestine.

11. The Death of Joshua

Read **Jos 24:29-33.**

Note: Chapter 24 of the Book of Joshua closes off a section of the Bible that some people like to call the *Hexateuch.* (Hexateuch = 6 scrolls). The *Hexateuch* covers Israel's religious history from the call of Abraham to the settlement in the promised land.

Look back to Unit 1, page 4 and revise what you learnt about the *Pentateuch.*

At Shechem, Joshua made it possible for the whole people of Israel to express its faith in God publicly and to renew its devotion to Him in a most solemn way. In the light of the dangers ahead, this ceremony had a deep meaning.

The Canaanite religion: Students of ancient times have found writings and small statues that tell quite a lot about the religion of the Canaanites. These people had male and female gods (*Baalim:* plural) who were worshipped *on the high places. Astarte (Astaroth:* plural) was their most important female god. Among the Canaanites, the main purpose of worship was to get the gods to give the gift of fertility to the soil, to animals and to people. Many of their religious ceremonies included practices like 'sacred' prostitution. The prostitutes were supposed to represent the goddess who, in turn, was supposed to have the power to give the gift of fertility.

How different all this was from the truth made known by the holy God of Israel, the Lord of Creation.

12. The Book of Judges

The information you have already been given about the Sinia and Shechem covenants, about the Holy War, and the Canaanite religion, should help you with the **Book of Judges.**

After the death of Joshua the people fell away from God and went after the fertility gods of the Canaanites. To punish them for this dreadful apostasy, God handed them over to enemies such as the Canaanites, Madianites, Philistines, etc. Whenever they repented, God raised up national heroes (the judges) to free them and to bring them back to the worship of the true God. Whenever this hero (or judge) passed on, they soon fell away again, so strongly were they attracted by this nature religion of the Canaanites.

In the **Book of Judges,** religious history follows this pattern:

Apostasy _ Punishment _ Repentance _ Deliverance.

This is how it goes: The Israelites began to displease God (apostasize) and He handed them over (to an enemy); they cried to the Lord and He raised up (a judge) to set them free. Then they began to displease the Lord —. Over and over, God's people had to be taught this same lesson: *You will not survive if you are unfaithful to your God.*

Read **Judg 2:6-23.**

a. How did God show His faithful love for the people? ________

b. How did the people show unfaithfulness and hard-heartedness towards God? ____

c. Why did God leave other nations in Canaan? ________

Some of the best known of the Judges were: *Deborah and Barak, Gideon, Samson.*

Read: **Judg 4 and 5:** Deborah and Barak
Judg 6 and 7: Gideon
Judg 13:1-8: Birth of Samson
Judg 16:23-31: Death of Samson

Samson's strength came from his consecration to God.

Note: **God, The Lord of History.** You have already seen how God mastered the Egyptians and other peoples who opposed the Israelites during the desert wanderings, and you know why God left different nations in the promised land. As you read more of the Bible and think about how God managed the nations, you should come to a strong realization that He is the *Lord of the nations* and the *God of history.*

d. Write down **Is 40:15.**

e. Read **Ps 136** in a prayerful way.

f. A prayer to learn:

Let us thank God for all the wonders of His love for us:
the wonder of creation;
the wonder of the departure from Egypt, which is a symbol of our baptism;
the wonder of His protection in the desert, which is an image of our life;
the wonder of the entry into the promised land, which is for us the holy Church of Our Lord Jesus Christ.

13. The Book of Ruth

The **Book of Ruth** refers to the time of the Judges, roughly 1,200 – 1,000 BC. It is a quiet story of ordinary people going about their daily life and it contrasts strongly with the Book of Judges which is so full of war and warnings.

Ruth was a girl from *the land of Moab* who married an Israelite. In time her husband died, and then, instead of going back to her own people, she went with her mother-in-law, Naomi, to the Land of Israel. God blessed this lovely girl so that she found peace and happiness among His People and, in the divine plan, her son was the grandfather of David, Israel's greatest king.

This book is especially beautiful for what it tells us about God. Yes, God is truly active in the lives of ordinary people and the little things that make up their lives are important to Him. He blesses them and takes them up into the heart of His great saving work.

Read the **Book of Ruth**.

It was quite right for the people of Israel to take pride in the fact that God chose them out of all the peoples of the earth for Himself. However, sometimes they overdid this, as for example when they went on to think that God has no love or care for other people.

The little story about Ruth, the *Moabite,* corrects this wrong idea and so does the **Book of Jonah,** which you can read now or leave for later on, if you wish.

- It is God's will that we Christians live among people with different beliefs and values from those given by Our Lord Jesus Christ. Let us try to see ourselves in the Chosen People, and to learn from their experience. We too, must take to heart the solemn warning of the Book of Judges: *you will not survive if you are unfaithful to your God.*

Write a prayer to God and ask Him to help you not to be drawn away from the Christian beliefs and values you have been given.

UNIT SIX
A king to rule over us

SAMUEL, the last of the Judges, was raised up by God to lead and guide the Israelites through a period of change. You know already that when they first went into Canaan, they settled down, tribe by tribe, in the part marked out for them. They were a people united under divine rule and by God's holy law. This is how it was for about two hundred years and then one day an official group came to Samuel at Ramah to ask him to appoint a king to govern them. No one knows all the reasons for this. The Bible does say that Samuel's sons were not fit to rule over the people. Also we know that the *Philistines* had become a danger to the whole of Israel, so maybe it was the right time for the tribes to come together under one leader. On the other hand, it is true that there was a drift away from God and that some people were not satisfied with the way He had arranged things for them. Samuel himself was very worried about the whole business; he talked it over with God and was told to give into the people and to anoint *Saul* as king of all Israel.

The new set-up brought to Israel so much that was good and so much that was bad, that it is really not possible to say straight out whether kingship was a good thing or not. Certainly, *very important religious ideas developed during the time of the kingship in Israel,* for example, ideas that prepared the way for the coming of the Saviour, for the Kingship of Jesus and for the Kingdom of God.

The Bible has kept two traditions about the appointment of an earthly king (or monarch) in Israel – one approves and the other does not. The question of the two traditions is tied to the more difficult question of who wrote (or compiled) the **Books of Samuel.** Biblical scholars tell us that a number of writers (or editors) had something to do with these books and to prove this they point to passages that somehow don't seem to follow on, for example:

1 Sm 10:1 says that Saul was anointed King by Samuel and **1 Sm 10:24** says that it was the people who made him king. In earlier units where we are dealing with other books, you were told how different traditions were handed down orally for a very long time before they were put into writing. This point about the *number of editors* is brought in here only to help you realize that the composition of most books of the Bible is not easy to explain. Some people who have studied the biblical texts very deeply know a great deal about them, but even so, there is always something they cannot explain and that is *God's part in the composition of the sacred text.*

Note: There are *four* books in the Bible that deal with the rise and history of the Kingdom of Israel. In some Bibles they are called:

1 Samuel; 2 Samuel; 1 Kings; 2 Kings

In others:
1 Kings; 2 Kings; 3 Kings; 4 Kings.
(In Unit 1 you learned about differences between the Jewish and the Greek Bible, see p.11.)

Many of the things in these four books were written down at the time, or at least very near the time, they happened . . . probably about a thousand years before Jesus was born. The court history of King David, **2 Sam 9 – 20** and **1 Kings 1 – 2** could have been written by an eye-witness.

1. Samuel: The last of the Judges

A. THE BIRTH OF SAMUEL

Read **1 Sam 1.**

a. Where did Elkhanah and his familylive? __________

b. Why did they go to Shiloh every year? __________

c. In her prayer Hannah asked God to *remember* her. What did she expect God to do? __________

d. What promise did Hannah make to God? (Among some people, not to cut their hair was a sign of consecration to God.) __________

B. SAMUEL AT SHILOH

Read **1 Sam 2:11-36.**

a. Why were Eli's sons described as worthless men? __________

b. How was Samuel different from Eli's sons? __________

c. Complete: Verse __________ to verse __________ tells about the punishment that was to come on Eli's family.

C. THE CALL OF SAMUEL

Read **1 Sam 3.**

a. Write down Samuel's answer to the Lord. __________

b. What reason did God give for punishing Eli's sons? __________

c. Why was Eli punished? __________

D. SAMUEL: JUDGE AND DELIVERER

Read **1 Sam 7:2-17.**

a. Why were the Israelites under the power of the Philistines? __________

b. Why did the Lord fight for the Israelites? ________

c. Complete: The sacred writer considers that Samuel was a good leader because ________

E. THE PEOPLE ASK FOR A KING

Read **1 Sam 8.**

a. Look closely at **verses 19,20** and think over these questions:
Who was Israel's king during the desert wanderings? ________
Who gave Israel a law to live by? ________
Who led Israel into battle in the time of the Judges? ________

b. How did God feel about the people's desire for a king? (see **v.7**) ________

c. From **v.18,** do you think that God would ever bring back the tribal way of life? ______

d. Once the Kingdom of Israel was set up, who would be responsible for the nation? ________

e. Which verse mentions Israel's sin of serving false gods? ________

In ancient times: In some nations kings were treated like gods. What a serious thing it would be if, at some time in the future, God's people were to copy them.

- How important it is for us *to see ourselves in the people of Israel!* Here they are now, these people chosen by God, marked as His very own (by circumcision) and bound to Him by a covenant, turning to Him and saying: "We want to be like other nations." Think! Do we sometimes turn on God after all He has done and say in our own way: "We want to be like other people!"
  e.g. We don't want the Church to tell us what to believe. No. We want to be like other people.
  We don't want to go to Mass on Sundays. No. We want to be like other people.

  f. Write an example of your own: "We ________

  g. Read **1 Pet 2:9-10** where St Peter explains what it means to be chosen by God and baptised into Christ. Try to learn these two verses off by heart; they tell us so clearly who we are and how much God has done for us.

2. King Saul

A. THE CALL AND ANOINTING OF SAUL

Read **1 Sam 9 and 10.**

Samuel realized that God was calling Saul to a special vocation. It is very beautiful to see how this holy old man respects God's choice and honours the one who will be responsible for God's people in the future.

a. Note down any verses in **Ch 9** that help us to realize that it was God who chose Saul. e.g. **v** ________, **v** ________

Chapter **10:1a** describes the anointing of Saul. In this ceremony, Saul stands before us in full view and all our attention is on him. Through the anointing with oil *God's spirit is given him* so that he becomes a leader who will *save* God's people.

b. Write out **1 Sam 10:1a** ________

- The Church carries on this sacred practice of anointing with oil. In baptism and confirmation, in the sacrament of the sick and in ordination of priests, the person is anointed with oil as a sign that he/she is receiving God's Holy Spirit.

c. The people of the Bible always looked for *signs* to tell them that God was acting in their history. How many signs did Samuel give Saul? (See **Ch 10**) ________

d. Read Samuel's last message to the people, **1 Sam 12.** Write out verses **14** and **25.** ________

B. SAUL AS KING

The young king Saul had many victories and the people were very proud of him. Several times he saved them from their enemies, but in God's eyes he was a failure and had to be put aside. God would find someone fit to take Saul's place.

a. Write out **1 Sam 13:14.** ________

b. Read **1 Sam 15:10-35.** (Remember one of the rules of the Holy War was that everything should be destroyed). Why did God put Saul aside? ________

Note: There were other things in Saul's behaviour that made him displeasing to God. For example, once he behaved as though he were priest and another time he tried to find out about the future by asking a witch to get in touch with the dead.

c. Read **1 Sam 28:3-25.** Write out **v.19.** ________

C. SOMEONE TO TAKE SAUL'S PLACE

God's free choice fell on the boy David of Bethlehem, a member of the tribe of Judah. Samuel was sent to anoint him as king in place of Saul.

a. Read **1 Sam 16:1-13.**

A long time passed and David had many adventures before he began to rule as King of Judah. You will enjoy reading the account of his victory over the powerful Philistine, *Goliath.*

As you see this brave, handsome young man going out alone to fight the great enemy, you can think of Jesus, braver and more handsome still, going out alone to fight and overcome the greatest enemies of all mankind . . . sin and death.

b. Read **1 Sam 17:41-54.**

D. THE DEATH OF SAUL

King Saul was killed in battle against the Philistines, just as Samuel had foretold. The account of his tragic death is in **1 Sam 31.** It is most noticeable that God is not mentioned at all in this chapter; you feel that He was not there when Saul died and credit is given to the idols of the Philistines for Israel's defeat. Right to the end, David respected Saul as the "Lord's anointed" and loved his son, Jonathan.

Read **1 Sam 31** and **2 Sam 1:17-27.**

3. King David

A. GOD'S SPIRIT IS WITH DAVID

Ever since his anointing, the Spirit of God has been with David helping him to grow in the ways of God. With outstanding courage and goodness, he came through many trials in the days when Saul was still King. (Some time you might like to read more about David's early life, **1 Sam 16f,** but for now let us go on with his kingship.) It took him *seven* years to win the support of all Israel. At first the people in the north of the country wanted one of Saul's sons as king and even went so far as to set him up in a safe place across the Jordan. Meanwhile, David was at Hebron ruling over the Southern part called *Judah.* When at last the northern tribes gave in and followed David, he moved to *Jerusalem* and made that city the *capital* and *religious centre* of his kingdom.

a. Read **2 Sam 2:1-7.**

b. Take time to study the map of *The United Kingdom of Israel* on p.60.

Note: **Burial** – Even though Saul died without honour, David was pleased that he was buried properly. Among the people of the Bible, to leave a body unburied was a sign that the dead person was completely worthless. When the prophet Jeremiah wanted to correct one of Israel's kings for his bad behaviour, he warned: "He will have the funeral honours of a donkey; he will be dragged away and thrown outside Jerusalem's gates" **Jer 22:19.** In each of the four Gospels there is quite a long passage about the burial of Jesus. As we read these sad passages, we get comfort from knowing that Jesus' holy body was treated with such reverent care.

c. Read **Jn 19:38-42.**

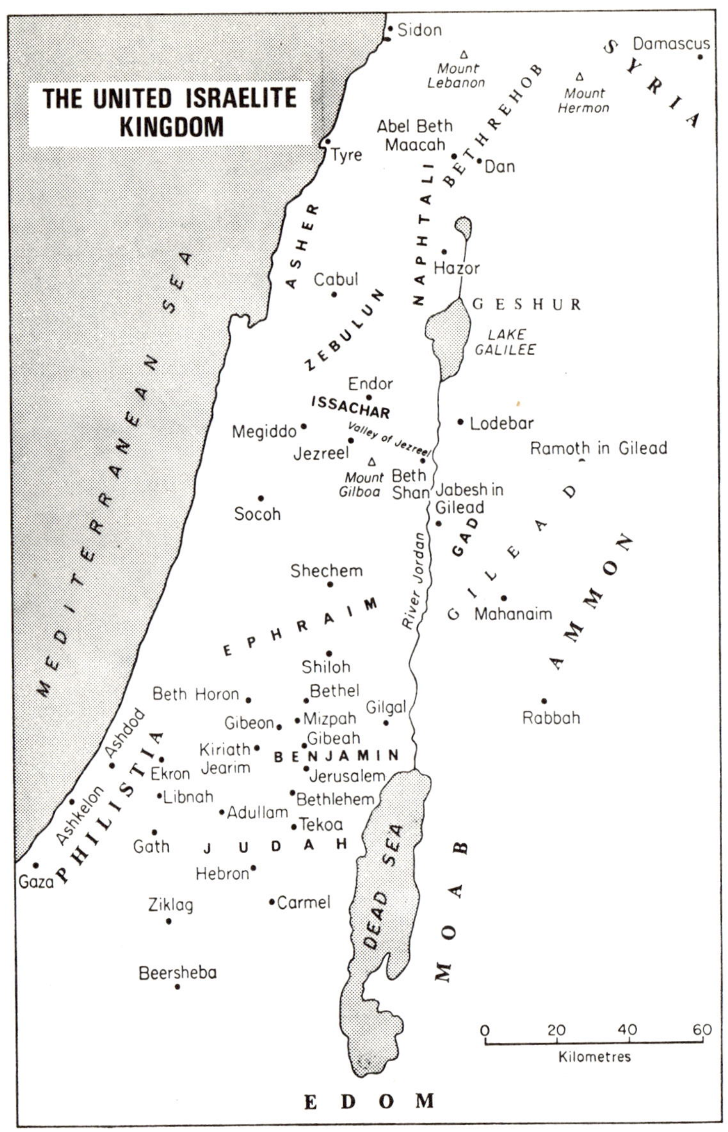

Map IV

The New Testament teaching about our bodies is truly amazing and no wonder the Church buries the faithful with such ceremony.

d. Write out **1 Cor 6:19-20.** __________

B. DAVID'S CARE FOR THE ARK OF THE LORD

Once David's kingdom was united and the Philistines had been beaten, David rested from war for a while and gave his attention to sacred worship. First, he had to think about the *Ark of the Lord* (covenant box) that the people had with them from the time they left Mt Sinai. This holy

Ark had had several resting places since the day it was first brought to the promised land. Really, you should go back and read the story of the capture of the Ark by the Philistines: **1 Sam Ch 4, 5, 6, 7:1** and then:

Read **2 Sam 6:1-15.**

Write the number of verse:
v. ________ tells of *joy* in the presence of God.
v. ________ tells of *reverence* in the presence of God.
v. ________ tells of *blessings* from the presence of God.

C. A SOLEMN PROMISE TO DAVID

Read **2 Sam 7.** (This is a very important chapter.)

Did you notice that God spoke to David through the *Prophet Nathan?* As you will see from the next unit, *prophets* had a very important part to play in the religious history of Israel during the period of the Kings which lasted for about five hundred years.

a. What did King David want to do for God? ________

b. Write out **v.16** which contains one of the great promises of the Old Testament. ____

For nearly 1,000 years, holy men and women in Israel lived by this *promise;* they *waited in faith* for its fulfilment. How carefully, and with what difficulty, they traced the line of King David's descendants, always wondering how it would be possible for David's kingdom to last forever. With deep disappointment, they found in most of his descendants only unfaithfulness to God and disrespect for His covenant and Law. From studying the events of their history and thinking deeply on the ways of God, they came to the belief that God would surely send someone who would be holy and powerful; who would purify their nation and save it by bringing it back into God's favour. This person, they called the **Messiah.** (In Hebrew *Messiah* = Anointed One; the Greek word for Messiah is *Christ.*) The *Messiah* would be a descendant of David and, like his great ancestor, he would save them from their enemies and set up a mighty kingdom of peace and holiness.

Psalm 132 recalls the *promise* made by God to David and points ahead to the coming of the *Messiah.*

c. Read **Ps132.**

d. Read **Lk 1:26-33.** Write out **vv. 32 & 33** ________

D. DAVID'S VICTORIES

Drawing on the old ideas of the holy war, the Sacred Writer shows us how greatly God blessed the Kingdom of Israel and how loyal David was to God and the covenant way of life. He tells us of the many battles won and of the new lands added to the Kingdom. Here are some of them:
Philistia; Moab; Edom; Ammom; Syria.
Find these countries on Map IV.

E. A TURNING POINT IN DAVID'S REIGN

Up to now, King David's reign has been glorious for Israel, but there are hard years ahead, years when members of David's own family will rise up and fight among themselves and try to take the kingship from David. In the sacred writer's mind, the root cause of all this trouble was *sin.*

Read **2 Sam 11.**

a. Complete: v. ________ to v. ________ tells of David's sin of adultery.
v. ________ to v. ________ tells of David's sin of dishonesty.

(If Uriah had gone home, he would have broken one of the rules for soldiers fighting a Holy War).

v. ________ to v. ________ tells of David's sin of murder.

In order to make David see his sin clearly, the prophet Nathan told him a special kind of story called a *parable.* (There are not many parables in the Old Testament, perhaps only ten, but in the New Testament you can find plenty "for Jesus often taught in parables".)

Read **2 Sam 12:1-25.**

b. Write down David's confession. ________

- When God forgives, He forgives fully; yet sin always leaves its mark; it always does some damage; we experience after-effects. This is a mystery and a burden, but it has a very good side too, because it opens our heart to God's mercy and helps us to grow in a spirit of repentance.

You can see from **Ps 51** how much David counted on God's mercy and how deeply repentant he was.

c. See how much of **Psalm 51** you can learn off by heart; make it one of your own prayers.

Sanctuaries: In all religions, people have places where they gather to worship their god and offer prayers. They think of the god as being present in these places; they mark them off as *sacred places* or sanctuaries. Usually a place became sacred because a god (or our God) made his presence felt there. Springs of water, high places or clumps of trees were likely to be sacred places. God's people had their sacred places. There were many of them and some more important than others. In these places they could worship God, and experience the saving events of their history, but they were forbidden to put up images of God there.

In the time of the patriarchs, *Bethel* was an important sanctuary; during the desert wanderings Israel's sanctuary was the *'Tent'* and in the land of Canaan before the building of the Temple, *Shiloh* was the main sanctuary. Often enough, the people of Israel seemed to take over sacred places from the Canaanites. This worried King David and so, in the hope of keeping his people clear of Canaanite religious practices, he closed down many sanctuaries. (That was not his only reason. He hoped to unite the people and to win their loyalty by bringing them regularly to *Jerusalem* to worship God in the holy sanctuary there, near his palace.)

4. King Solomon

A. SOLOMON'S REIGN

When David was very old, his son Solomon was anointed King of Israel by Nathan the prophet. You can read David's last instructions to Solomon in **1 Kings 2:1-9.**

a. What three things did David tell Solomon to do? ________
(Notice that two of them seem to be connected in some way with his sin).

Solomon's reign began very well. God gave him the gift of wisdom to rule wisely; there was peace and wealth in the Kingdom.

b. Read **1 Kings 3:4-15.**

One of his greatest works was to build the Temple for the Lord in Jerusalem.

The description of the Temple is written in a way that makes it easy for us to have strong and reverent feelings for this beautiful and holy building which was really only a shadow of the beauty and holiness of God. It was a glorious day for all Israel when the holy Ark of the Lord was brought in triumph into Solomon's Temple. From that day until the total destruction of Jerusalem in 587 B.C. the Temple of Solomon had a most important and privileged place in the life of God's people. **Ps 84** expresses the feelings many people had for this House of God which was *a symbol of God's presence* among his people.

c. Read **1 Kings 5 and 6.**

d. Read **Ps 84.**

B. A SAD END

After some years, Solomon became unfaithful to God. First he disobeyed God by marrying foreign women and then, to please them, had temples built for their gods. With his permission and help, idolatry was practised right in the heart of God's holy city.

Read **1 Kings 11:1-13.**

a. What reason did God give for taking away the Kingdom from Solomon? ________

b. How did God make it known that He was remembering His Promise to David? ____

As a result of King Solomon's sin several enemies rose up against Israel and a Prophet told in a symbolic way what God intended to do in Israel and why.

Read **1 Kings 11:26-40.**

c. Name the foreign gods who were honoured in Jerusalem. ________

The sacred writer ends his record of Solomon's reign quite suddenly. You see, in his mind, it is how a person stands with God that really matters; other things do not count for much.

Read **1 Kings 11:41 -43.**

C. A LIVING TEMPLE

Solomon's Temple in Jerusalem had a special place in the life and history of Israel. The history of all the people is closely linked with the history of the Temple. Later, you will hear how it was destroyed in 587 B.C. and how another one was built in place of it. It was this second Temple that Jesus knew so well and visited often during His life-time; this Temple was destroyed also, not many years after the Ascension of Jesus.

a. Read **Lk 19:41-45.**

Why was the second Temple destroyed? ________

Note: Temples were made of stone and the main stones were the strong ones at ground level at the corners. They were called *corner-stones.* These carefully chosen stones held the walls of the building together.

One day in the Temple itself, Jesus added a new religious idea to those the people already had about the Temple.

b. Read **Jn 2:13-22.**

Write out **Jn 2:21.** ________

- In the new covenant times in which we live, the risen body of Jesus is the new spiritual temple where we worship God "in spirit and in truth". All those who believe in Him and are baptised in His name are living stones in this spiritual temple and Jesus is the *corner-stone* holding the believers together.

c. Read **Eph 2:19-22.**
Read **1 Pet 2:4-6.**

d. Write a prayer thanking Jesus for making you part of the living temple of the new covenant.

D. THE WISDOM OF SOLOMON

The Bible praises and admires Solomon as the wisest man in Israel. Besides using his gift of wisdom in ruling his Kingdom, Solomon shared it with others by encouraging them to study this deep question: What makes man's life good and happy?

In the Bible, there are *five* books that are especially concerned with the answer to this question. They are know as the **Wisdom Books** and they are: **Job, Proverbs, Ecclesiastes,**

Ecclesiasticus, and **Wisdom.** The style of writing in the 'Wisdom' Books consists mainly of sayings or pieces of advice put in a way that makes them easy to remember. For example:

"Without wood, a fire goes out; without gossip, quarrelling stops" **Pr 26:20.**

"Better to be poor and honest, than rich and dishonest" **Pr 28:6.**

Like the Israelites, other ancient peoples had their books of wisdom and these resemble those of the Bible, *but there is a real difference* because the wise men of Israel knew what God had made known about Himself and about man and they based their study on this. In time, as God revealed more and more to them, they came to realize that true wisdom is knowing, loving and serving God and that reverence for God is the foundation for this.

a. Choose from the Book of Proverbs one saying that you think would help you to live a better life, and write it down. ________

UNIT SEVEN
Prophets and kings

Background: When King Solomon died, his son *Rehoboam* became king. He treated the people so badly that soon there was a revolt in the kingdom. The Northern tribes broke away; they made *Jeroboam* their King and *Shechem* their capital. (Later on the capital was moved to *Tirzah* and finally to *Samaria.* Only the tribe of Judah stayed with *Rehoboam.* From this time onward, the *Kingdom was divided* and so we must now speak *of the Northern part* as the **Kingdom of Israel** and the *Southern part* as the **Kingdom of Judah**.
To stop his people from going down to Jerusalem (many people loved to go to the Temple) the King of Israel set up two sanctuaries in his kingdom, one at *Bethel* and one at *Dan* and told them to worship in these places. (Do you remember why King David closed down sanctuaries and brought the people to Jerusalem? See pp.62-3.)

1. Division in Israel

Take time to study Map V, on p.67. Look at:
— the boundaries
— the names of surrounding countries
— the names of the towns and villages.

Read **1 Kings 12**

a. Even though the revolt against Rehoboam is explained in a natural way, there is one verse that shows us clearly that God is Lord of history. Which one is it? __________

b. Write out Shemaiah's message to Rehoboam. __________

c. Jeroboam did several things that caused the people to turn away from God. What were they? __________

Background: After the division of the kingdom, the lands that David added to it broke away and became enemies once more. Only very rarely did Israel and Judah support each other; more often they wore each other down by fighting. There were like two jealous sisters.

In many ways the two kingdoms were different. Judah was small and rather poor, but her people were fairly united. She did not have very much contact with other nations and her king was always a descendant of King David. Israel was larger and richer than Judah; her people were not as united and they had more contact with other nations. Several different families

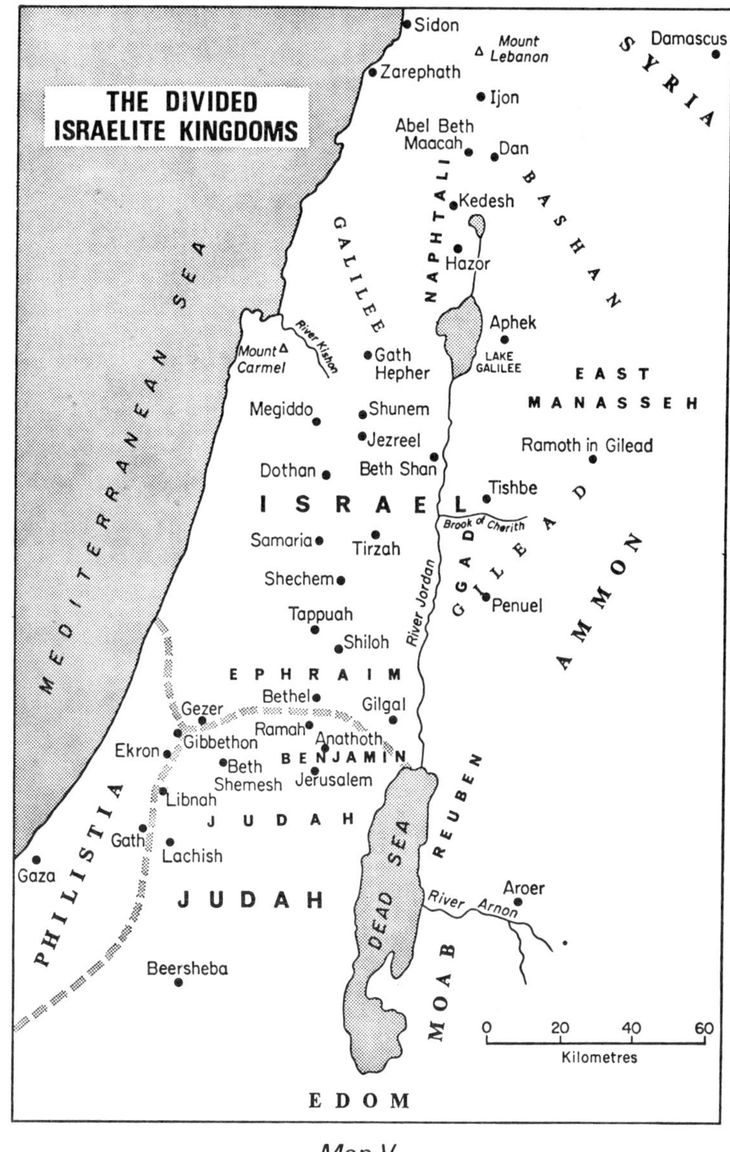

Map V

rose up and claimed the throne. For these reasons, the history of the two kingdoms was different. Because of her circumstances, it was perhaps easier for Judah to be faithful to God than it was for Israel, and she lasted longer. However, the Bible says that both were destroyed *because they were unfaithful to God and to the covenant way of like.*

Knowing that Israel and Judah were destroying themselves by their sins, God in His loving-kindness *sent great prophets* to His people in both kingdoms. These prophets were *called by God* to speak His thoughts and to express His feelings. In answer to God's call, they did all they could to get the whole nation to turn to God again and be saved. In God's Name they worked miracles, gave signs of things to come, prayed, suffered, advised kings, taught, corrected, warned, encouraged, etc. But there were very few kings, especially in Israel, who took any notice of the prophets; many of them drove them away and caused them to suffer.

In the **Book of Kings** the sacred writer has summed up the reigns of the different Kings of Israel and Judah. Even though some of them were successful from a wordly point of view, for example *Omri* in Israel, the sacred writer does not praise them; he is interested only in how they kept the covenant and what worship was like during their reign. Often he ends his short note on a king with these words: "He did what was displeasing to God." Whenever we read this remark, we know that idolatry was strong and that the king either did nothing to stop it or actually made it worse.

2. Notes on Kings

Read **1 Kings 16:23-28; 1 Kings 16:29-34; 2 Kings 16:1-5; 2 Kings 18:1-7.**

a. How did Ahab compare with the other Kings of Israel? ________

b. Why was Ahab's marriage to Jezebel a bad thing for Israel? ________

c. What did Ahaz do that made him displeasing to God? ________

d. Why does the sacred writer praise King Hezekiah? ________

3. The Prophet Elijah

God sent the great prophet Elijah to Israel in the bad days when Ahab was king, 869 – 850 B.C. He was the only prophet at that time who stood up for the worship of the true God of Israel. (There were plenty of false prophets around; these had not been called by God; they were for Baal.)

Read **1 Kings 18:20-40.**

a. Consider this question: Did Elijah believe that Baal really existed? ________

Jezebel hated Elijah because he shamed her god, Baal. She intended to get even with him, but he escaped into the desert and went back to Mt Sinai.

In both kingdoms, in the future, one of the hardest tasks of all will be to keep true religion alive among God's people. This is why Elijah's visit to Mt Sinai at this time has such a deep meaning. By going back to the place where the religion of Israel began, he stirs up memories and brings back that first, true understanding of what the call and vocation of Israel meant.

Read **1 Kings 19:1-18.**

b. In the time of war and trouble that is coming whom will God save? ________

- Elijah's journey through the desert to Mt Sinai reminds us of the forty days Jesus spent in the desert preparing for His saving work. It also reminds us of the time of Lent when we prepare ourselves to share in the saving mysteries of Jesus at Easter. In the desert, Jesus found life and strength in doing the will of His Father; for our journey into eternity, we find life and strength in the Word of God and in the Eucharist.

c. Look up **Lk 4:1-15.**

d. Write out **Jn 4:34.**

● On Mt Sinai, Moses met God and their meeting was marked by thunder and lightning. Elijah also met God in this holy place and their meeting was marked by the calm of a gentle breeze. When salvation history is complete, all mankind will meet God in His divine Son, Jesus, the One Who is "gentle and humble of heart".

4. The Prophet Elisha

The prophet Elisha was respected in the kingdom of Israel and, during his lifetime, the lesson begun under Elijah went on slowly, namely: *It is foolish indeed not to listen to God's prophets.* Elijah took off his cloak and put it on Elisha. This was the sign that Elijah's prophetic power had passed on to Elisha. In **2 Kings 4:1 – 8:15** there is a collection of miracle-stories connected with Elisha (or with his disciples). These stories help us to realize the greatness of the prophet Elisha whose kindness went out to all, even to the enemies of Israel.

a. Read **2 Kings 4:8-37; 2 Kings 5:1-15.**

There are many miracle-stories in the Gospels. These show Jesus' divine power over nature, sickness, death, evil spirits and sin.

b. Read **Lk 5:12-16; Lk 7:11-17.**

Elijah and Elisha did their work for God rather like soldiers or rebels. Perhaps they thought that the way to defeat idolatry and bring the people back to God was to set up a new ruling family (or dynasty). The great prophets who came later saw that changing the ruling family was not the way to bring about faithfulness to God. They acted more like teachers, or reformers hoping that throught their teaching and example the whole nation would turn and come back to God.

Note: In the time of Samuel, when kingship was set up in Israel, everyone understood that the King had a special responsibility before God for the nation and that everything would go well if only he kept his people faithful to God. Each king was supposed to be so close to God that he would know God's thoughts and feelings and pass them on to the people. When a few good people in Israel thought deeply about this, they realized that kings were supposed to be *prophetic persons* and that kingship had not turned out the way God meant it to; that the struggle between kings and prophets was not part of His divine plan. This thought came to them: *If only someone would come who would be a prophet as well as a king!* And so a new hope centred on the coming of a **prophet-king** began to grow up among them. This *prophet-*

king would lead the nation in God's ways and it would be safe and at peace.

After almost eight hundred years of waiting, God did send the prophet-king to His people and it was the men and women of New Testament times who recognized and welcomed Jesus as this prophet-king.

c. Read **Mt 21:1-11; Jn 12:44-50.**

d. Write a short prayer thanking Jesus for making the thoughts and feelings of God known among us. __________

Background: About the middle of the 8th century BC Israel and Judah began to get rich. One of the reasons for this was that the *Assyrians,* a powerful nation, had put down some of their enemies. Now that they did not have to worry so much about preparing for war, many of God's people put their minds on making money. Some of their leaders also thought it would be a wise move to make friends with countries that might save them if a powerful nation like *Assyria* or *Egypt* were to come against them. It was this concern of theirs for making money and making friends that had a big part in their destruction.

Many thought that wealth was the most important thing in life and that only people with money counted. Divine election was no longer important in their eyes and so they did not respect the poor. In their greed, the rich robbed from the poor and even paid judges to hand down rulings against them. How far all this was from the way God had taught them to think and act!

This spirit of greed and dependence on other nations that spread among God's people had serious effects on their religion. They got into the way of thinking that religion had nothing to do with every day life and that all they had to do was to worship in the sanctuaries or Temple on sabbath and festival days; nor did it worry them that pagan practices were becoming part of their worship of God. With all their wealth and with all their friends and their splendid Temple they were certain that they had nothing to fear. Only very few people realized that underneath this great show things were going badly and that one day, God, the Lord of history, would call up a strong nation to punish them for the things they were doing.

These few people were God's servants, the prophets:
Amos; Hosea; Isaiah; Micah; Jeremiah

- God told Moses – *"I, the Lord, am a God who is full of compassion and pity, who is not easily angered and who shows great love and faithfulness. I keep my promise for thousands of generations and forgive evil and sin: but I will not fail to punish . . . ".*

All the prophets shared this same understanding of God and that is why they spoke in the way they did.

God's punishment is only for people who show no sorrow for their sins and choose to go on doing them.

5. The Prophet Amos

Amos, a shepherd from Judah, saw clearly what an evil thing greed is and felt very strongly about the unjust way the rich treated the poor. He knew that God wanted him to speak out about what he saw and so he went to the Northern Kingdom, to the famous shrine at *Bethel,* to protest there. Jeroboam II was king at that time. He reigned from 786 – 746 BC. (By now the capital had been moved to Tirzah.)

Read **Amos 7:10-17.**

a. Write out the verse that tells us that Amos was sure of his call to the prophecy. ____

b. Which verse tells us that there were false prophets in Israel? __________

c. What reason did the priest of Bethel give for sending Amos away? __________

ISRAEL'S SINS

Read **Amos 8:4-14**

d. Complete: v. __________ tells of injustice.
v. __________ tells of dishonesty.
v. __________ tells of pretence at worship.
v. __________ tells of idolatry.

These sins are named in **Amos 2:6-8** and the reasons why they are so terrible in God's eyes are given in **Amos 2:9-11.**

Read **Amos 2:6-11.**

e. Why is God so disappointed in His People? __________

Amos 3:2a gives the deepest reason of all why God is so upset about the unfaithfulness of Israel.

f. Write out **3:2a.** __________

In the hope that His people would turn away from their sins, God gave them several warnings, but they did not take any notice of these. They went on sinning with never a thought for God's justice.

Read **Amos 4:4-12.**

g. Write down three warnings that God gave. __________

Note: **The Day of the Lord**

On page 48 you learnt about the holy war. Remember how every victory was counted as a victory for God. Whenever a battle was won, the people would say: This is a Day of the Lord and they expected that one day God would show the full extent of His power and justice by defeating all their enemies, and especially *Assyria.* They could hardly wait for this day to come; they referred to it as "the Day of the Lord", and of course, they expected to share in God's glorious victory!

Many of Israel's prophets took up this idea of "the day of the Lord". They told the people – Yes, you are right, the day of the Lord is coming and *you had better look out* because there will be a new kind of victory on that day. It will not be a victory over nations: it will be a victory over *sin.* They said it would not be a day of celebration for the chosen people, but a dreadful day of punishment because of the wicked, sinful way *they* were living.

Even though the prophets often spoke in a frightening way, deep in their hearts there was a great love for their own people; they wished that they would listen and turn back to God so that they would be *saved* on "the day of the Lord".

Read **Amos 5:18-20,** where he describes "the day of the Lord".
Read **Amos 4:1-3.**

h. To whom is he speaking? ________

Read **Amos 6**

i. What lesson did Amos expect the people to learn from the destruction of Calneh, Ḥamath and Gath? ________

Amos knew in his heart that his prayers and efforts would be wasted on Israel because the people were proud and hard-hearted. He knew that they would experience the full justice of God on "the day of the Lord".

Read **Amos 8:2-3.**

With his understanding of God's ways, Amos was able to look beyond the day of destruction to a *beautiful time when God would make everything right again for His People.*

Read **Amos 9:11-15.**

Note: Not only Amos, but the other prophets too saw beyond the time of hardship and punishment to a time when God would visit His people in mercy and love. Then He would give them peace and make them safe and happy once more in their own land. They called this time, *a time of* **restoration.** And so, through the prophets, another fresh hope took root in the hearts of a few good people: In His own time *God will make everything right for us.* These two ideas: **destruction** (because of God's justice) and **restoration** (because of God's faithful love) run through the sayings of the prophets.

From the time of the prophets onward, we find a small number of good people waiting for and wondering about the **restoration.** True enough, a restoration did come in the history of the chosen people when God brought them back to Israel from Babylon where they had been taken as prisoners. We will learn about this restoration in the next unit. It was a wonderful event, but still only a shadow of the *final restoration* in which all mankind shares.

- By their sin, Adam and Eve destroyed man's peace with God. Through His saving mysteries Jesus *restored* man's *peace* with God. All salvation history leads up to this great and final *restoration.*

6. The Prophet Hosea

The prophet Hosea was called by God to preach in the Northern Kingdom and he was there to see the words of Amos come true.

Yes, about twenty years after the death of King Jeroboam II, "the day of the Lord" came.

After King Jeroboam II's death in 746 B.C. things went from bad to worse. The people fought among themselves; they murdered their kings; violence and greed and injustice were everywhere; there was no end to it.

Meanwhile, *Assyria* had grown strong under a new leader called Pul. (His other name was Tiglath-Pileser III.) At first Israel tried to keep in with Assyria by paying out large sums of money every year, and when they could no longer raise the money, they tried to get a number of small nations, including Judah, to join together and attack Assyria. Although these and other plans for saving themselves failed, they still had no thought of turning to God for help.

The prophet Hosea was deeply upset at seeing his own dear land going to ruin and *all because it was unfaithful to the covenant made long ago on Mt Sinai.*

On "the day of the Lord" their beautiful city, Samaria, which King Omri had made the capital, was destroyed and the people were taken off as prisoners. This was the year 721 B.C.

Hosea himself was a very loving person; he wanted only to spare his people much suffering. Most of all, he wanted to spare God's feelings for he knew how He suffered at seeing His own chosen people unfaithful in so many ways – honouring other gods, offering them presents, trusting in money and in friends who did not really love them and living in a way that brought disgrace on Him in the eyes of other nations. Knowing the loving heart of God so well, Hosea was certain that everything would be all right if the people would just turn back to God and to the way of life He had set out for them.

Hosea had a very sad experience in his own life. He fell in love with a prostitute named Gomer and married her. He thought that since he loved her so much, she would change and never go back to her old ways. Even though she disappointed him, he never lost his love for her. Time and again, he would go and bring her back and he was never harsh or rough with her. When all her lovers grew tired of her and she was in slavery, he went and paid for her freedom and took her back as his wife. Yet she never loved him in return.

When Hosea thought about his unhappy marriage, he saw that it was a picture of God's covenant with Israel. Just as the wife he loved so much was unfaithful to him, so the people God loved as His own were unfaithful to Him.

Israel's behaviour.

Read: **Hosea 3**: Israel acts like an unfaithful wife.
Hosea 4:1-4: Israel's sins.
Hosea 4:11-14: Israel trusts in other gods.
Hosea 5:4-8: Israel loves other gods.
Hosea 7:1-3; 11:1-5: Israel turns away from God's love.
Hosea 7:8-16: Israel trusts in other nations.

Punishment
Hosea told the people of Israel exactly what their punishment would be. God, the Lord of Nations would "use" other nations as a means of punishing them.

Read **Hos 9:1-7; Hos 11:5-8.**

a. Which nations will God use to punish Israel? ________

b. How will these nations punish Israel? ________

Restoration
Hosea knew that God's love is everlasting and that He could never give up His people; that He could never forget them. He was sure that a time would come when God would bring them back to their own land and fill them with His blessings.

Read **Hos 11:8-10; 14:4-9**

Read **Ps 136** in a prayerful way to thank God for making the mystery of His love for man known in so many ways and especially for not being ashamed to ask for our love in return.

7. The Prophet Isaiah

Introduction: The prophet Isaiah had such an active part in the making of Judah's history that it is not possible to write a short background history to his life as it was for Amos and Hosea. He said many of the things that they said about the unholy way God's people were living and like them spoke about *punishment* and *restoration.* He said Judah would be like a tree that is cut down and later sends up new growth from the small stump that was left. This "new growth" would come from a small group of faithful people whom God would save and this group would be able to trace its line back to King David.

Read: **Is 5:8-30**: The bad things that God's people were doing.
Is 3:16-25: The women did not care about religion.
Is 11:1-16: Punishment and Restoration.

Isaiah Ben Amoz was a statesman whom God called to be a prophet. This was in the year 742 BC, the same year that King Uzziah died. He had been king of Judah for 52 years. People remembered all the trouble there was in the Northern Kingdom when the long reign of Jeroboam II ended and they were afraid that the same thing would happen now in Judah.

Isaiah must have been in the Temple one day worrying about the future of Judah, for it was there God make known to him in a vision that the strength of the kingdom of Judah was not in earthly kings, but in Him, the Holy One, who was there among His people, ruling them from His throne in the temple.

Read **Is 6:1-8.**

Isaiah was active for at least forty years and, as a statesman and prophet, offered advice to several kings – probably to Jotham, Ahaz, Hezekiah and Manasseh. During these years, there was often pressure on Judah to go for help to other nations. Isaiah stood out against this; he would tell the kings: Keep out of other nations; don't get caught up in their plans. Always, his advice was based on his strong belief that God was Judah's true king; that He could take care of Judah and that He would be faithful to the promise He had made to King David: "You will always have descendants and I will make your kingdom last forever. Your dynasty will never end" **2 Sam 7:16**.

Ahaz was king of Judah when the northern king and his friend the King of Syria, came down to punish Judah for not joining them against Assyria. The young king Ahaz took fright. Read what he did and what Isaiah said to try to calm him down.

Read **2 Kgs 16:3-4**: King Ahaz took fright.
Is 7:1-9: Isaiah gave Ahaz advice.

Ahaz took no notice of Isaiah's advice. He invited Assyria to come in and protect him. Of course he would have to pay large sums of money to Assyria and besides this, give a place of honour to the gods of Assyria in the Temple of the Holy One of Israel. (Isaiah liked to call God "The Holy One.")

Even when people told Isaiah about the cruel things the Assyrians were doing in what had been the northern kingdom, he stood by the advice he had always given. He did not lose faith in God. As a statesman, he knew that this trouble would pass and, as a prophet, he believed that God would remember His promise to the House of David and send Judah a perfect king . . . one who would be wise and strong; who would love his people and bring them peace. This king would be the 'anointed one' of God, His Messiah.

Read **Is 7:10-17; Is 9:6-8.**

You have already been introduced to the idea of the coming of a Messiah. The more the few faithful people thought about this future Messiah, the more their hope and desire for him deepened. The one who expressed this best of all was Mary of Nazareth, who became the Mother of God.

Read **Lk 1:46-55.**

- Every year in Advent, the Church helps us to live again the long years of waiting for the coming of the Messiah and to welcome Him on Christmas night.

A prayer to learn

Come Lord Jesus,
do not delay;
give new courage to your people who trust in your love.
By your coming, raise us to the joy of your kingdom,
where you live and reign with the Father and the Holy Spirit,
one God forever and ever. Amen.

When Ahaz died, *Hezekiah* became king. He made a real effort to bring the people back to the true worship of God. (You could read **2 Kgs 18:1-7** again.)

When Hezekiah removed the Assyrian gods from the Temple, people saw two meanings in this action – a religious one, meaning that there was to be no more idolatry in Judah and a national one, meaning Judah was no longer going to depend on Assyria. Many of the King's advisers were pleased with the idea of not serving Assyria any more, but still they wanted to be sure of help from outside. On their advice, King Hezekiah made friends with Egypt. In spite of clear warnings from Isaiah, the King joined with Egypt and went ahead preparing for war against Assyria. As a statesman, Isaiah judged Egypt to be a weak partner and, as a prophet, he condemned God's people for trusting in a foreign nation instead of in their own great and holy God.

Read **Is 31:1-6.**

Hezekiah must have been very sorry that he did not follow Isaiah's advice. Listen to what happened as the Assyrian army led by King Sennacherib moved towards Jerusalem.

Read **Is 10:28-34.**

In great fear, Hezekiah went to Isaiah for special advice.

Read **Is 36:1 – 37:8.**

By now the Assyrians were all around Jerusalem. It was the year 701 B.C.; Sennacherib wrote this in his report: "I imprisoned him (Hezekiah) in Jerusalem, his residence, like a bird in a cage. I surrounded him with earthworks . . . ".

No one knows why, but at the last minute, Sennacherib called his soldiers off and Jerusalem was saved! God's prophet was right!

Manasseh became king after Hezekiah. You can read about him in **2 Kgs 21:1-19**. It is thought that Isaiah was killed during his reign.

Read **2 Kgs 21:1-19.**

8. The Prophet Micah

The Prophet Micah was active in Judah at the same time as Isaiah, but his ministry was not as long. He was a gardener (or small farmer) and he gave God's message in a very plain-spoken way. He realized that there were many things wrong with God's people, and told them so. He knew that God had called him to be a prophet and he was full of confidence in the power God had given him. He saw that the people were quite happy to follow bad leaders and false prophets and that greed and injustice were everywhere. He was amazed to find that people, who should have known better, had no sense of religion at all.

Read **Mic 1:1** : Micah's call.
3:8-12 : Micha spoke with confidence.
3:1-5 : Micah spoke against bad leaders.

Read **Mic 3:6-8** : Micah spoke against false prophets.
2:1-3 : Micah condemned greed and injustice.
6:6-9 : Micah explained the meaning of religion.
2:3-5 : Micah spoke of punishment.
7:8-13 : Micah spoke of restoration.
5:7 : Micah spoke of a faithful few from whom new life would come.

a. Write out and learn: **Mic 6:8.**

b. Write out and learn: **Mic 5:7**

9. The Prophet Jeremiah

Probably more is known about Jeremiah than about any other prophet because there is so much about him in the Book that has his name.

Jeremiah was a priest from Anathoth, a village near Jerusalem, and he received his call from God about the year 626 BC. He was a gentle person with a great love for God and for his own people, and yet he was made to suffer very much. There were times when he broke down altogether in the presence of God and gave out his deepest feelings. As we read some of these passages, we cannot help but think of Our Blessed Lord Himself.

Read **Jer 1:1-10**: The Call of Jeremiah.
Jer 11:18 – 12:7: The Sufferings of Jeremiah.

a. Look up **Mt 27:30-44.**
Mt 22:15-22

b. Complete: Jeremiah and Jesus suffered because __________

In the same year that Jeremiah received his call from God something happened that was very important for Judah. It was this. Babylonia, a country that had been part of the great Assyrian Empire broke away and soon developed into a strong nation. This made three great nations now in the ancient east: Assyria, Egypt, and Babylonia. Each watched the other carefully for fear of war.

It was hard for small nations to know what to do; they were worried about their freedom and safety. Sometimes their leaders could not agree about what would be best for them. In Judah, for example, there were leaders who wanted to depend on Assyria; others said, No, Egypt is more reliable. Since both Assyria and Egypt were against Babylonia, Judah could easily make herself an enemy of Babylonia. It was a very tricky situation. If Isaiah had been alive what advice do you think he would have given Judah?

When King Josiah was old enough to take charge of his country, he began to put an end to the harm done by Manasseh and his son, Amon. He tried to stop idolatry and to get rid of pagan ideas and practices. He repaired the Temple and made it *the* place of worship. Fortunately, too, he was able to free himself from the Assyrians without turning them into enemies.

Read **2 Kgs 23:4-27.**

Jeremiah must have looked with pleasure on all that Josiah was doing for the religion of God, but he realized that what was needed most of all was a *change of heart in everyone.* He told the people, God knows what you are doing and He will allow a foreign country to come from the north to punish you. A "boiling pot" that Jeremiah saw made him think of the plans great nations were "boiling up". Soon a strong nation would "spill over" into Israel.

Read **Jer 1:11-16.**

Jeremiah always gave his message in a strong poetic way. **Ch 2** is a good example of his style of preaching.

Read **Jer 2.**

It happened that while the Temple was being repaired, workmen found a very important book containing the Law of Moses. Most likely it had been hidden in the time Manesseh was king. The people were very excited about finding this old and sacred book. Maybe they took it as a sign that God was very pleased with them for repairing the Temple. Jeremiah warned them that having the Book of the Law would do them no good at all unless their lives matched what was laid down in it.

Read **Jer 5:1-12; Jer 11:1-9.**

The Death of King Josiah

By the year 612 BC the Babylonians were strong enough to capture Nineveh, the capital of Assyria. The Egyptians wanted to help the Assyrians against the Babylonians and this meant that they had to pass through Palestine. It is not clear what King Josiah thought about this, but it seems that he was afraid that if Assyria and Egypt defeated Babylonia, Egypt would take control of Palestine. It is thought that he set out with an army to block the Egyptians and that he was killed in a battle that took place at Megiddo.

(If you like, you can read the story of the fall of the city of Nineveh in the **Book of Nahum, Chapter 2.** It is seen as a punishment from God because Assyria had grown so proud and cruel and it teaches us that all nations must answer to God for what they do.)

The death of Josiah meant that all his plans for bringing the people of Judah back to God were cut off. His son, Jehoiakim was not a religious man and in a very short time all the old bad things were back again . . . injustice, greed, violence, idolatry. Jeremiah had plenty to protest about and in doing so, he made himself an enemy of King Jehoiakim.

Read **Jer 22:13-20.**

One day, with great courage, Jeremiah stood up in the Temple and said that the whole nation was so wicked that the city of Jerusalem and the Temple would be destroyed. It would be broken into pieces like a clay pot.

Read **Jer 7:1-16; Jer 19:1-16.**

Because of what Jeremiah had said about the future of the Temple, he was not allowed to preach in it anymore. But the people had to hear God's message! Now Jeremiah got everything he wanted to say written on a scroll and sent his secretary to the Temple to read it out aloud there. When news of this reached the king, he asked for the scroll. He was sitting by the fire in his winter palace when one of his officials brought it to him. He listened, and, as each column was read, he cut it off with a small knife and dropped it into the fire. That was all he cared about God's message to Judah!

Read **Jer 36:1-4, 20-25.**

Time passed and by 605 BC it was quite clear to Jeremiah that Babylonia was the nation that would come in from the north to punish Judah for her sins.

As King Nebuchadnezzar of Babylonia was not ready to come at once to take control of Judah, he told other nations like Moab and Syria, to go in and worry Judah. He would come himself when he was ready . . . and sure enough he did. One thing he did to weaken Jerusalem was to take away to the city of Babylon the leading people and all their skilled workers and all their valuable things. Those who were left behind in Jerusalem thought that they would never see these people again. Only Jeremiah thought differently; *he saw that the hope of the future was with these people.* A young priest called Ezekiel was among them.

After this first experience with King Nebuchadnezzar, you would think that Judah, small and poor as she was, would keep quiet and do as the Babylonians wanted. But nothing of the sort! Certain false prophets stirred up the hope that Judah would soon be free and that the prisoners would come back. Jeremiah said that this was nonsense, and he even wrote a letter to the prisoners in Babylon telling them to settle down and accept what had happened; they would certainly be there for a long time.

Jeremiah gave this advice because he knew his people were so set in their sinful ways and that it would take them a very long time to learn the old lesson: *You will not survive, if you are unfaithful to God.*

Read **Jer 29:1-24.**

By now, Zedekiah was king of Judah. He was a weak leader and gave too much power to his advisers whose one aim was to get back their freedom. They were always looking for a chance to rebel against Babylonia. Zedekiah often asked Jeremiah for advice, but never followed it.

Read **Jer 38:14-28.**

When Judah's leaders thought that the time was right, they rose up in rebellion against Babylonia. When this happened the great Babylonian army moved quickly in to Palestine, destroying all before it. Finally it reached the holy city itself. Although the people in Jerusalem fought bravely for several months, the Babylonians finally broke down the walls and got into the city. How they punished Judah! Truly, it was "the Day of the Lord"! Many people were murdered and many others were taken away as prisoners to Babylon. Important buildings, including the Temple, were robbed and them burned. *It was the year 587 BC.*

Read **Jer 52.**

The Babylonians were friendly towards Jeremiah because he never supported the rebellion. (Like Amos he believed that God's people were too hard-hearted to turn away from sin; that they would have to experience God's justice first before they would be ready to accept His mercy and love.)

Read **Jer 40:1-7.**

Jeremiah stayed in Judah for a while, perhaps for a few months, and after that he was taken to Egypt.

Read **Jer 43.**

Most of Jeremiah's preaching is heavy with warnings of destruction. He saw that the things that had united Israel to God in the past would be wiped out. These were kingship; the Temple; the Ark and priestly instruction. In spite of this, he believed that the worship of God would go on and that God would never forget the people He had chosen as His own. When he looked back over the history of Israel, Jeremiah came to this conclusion: His people would never manage to keep their side of the Sinai covenant and God would make a new kind of covenant so that it would be possible for them to be His people forever and for Him to be their God. This new covenant would be the greatest proof of God's love; *it* would be the means of restoration.

In this new covenant, God's commandments would be written in the hearts of His people; He would forgive their sins and give them a heart that would be ready to love and serve Him.

Read **Jer 24:4-8; Jer 31:31-35.**

- At the Last Supper, Jesus brought in this new covenant. He is God's Word to each of us and through Him we are able to love and serve God and have our sins forgiven. Through Jesus, all mankind receives a new heart and is formed forever into the People of God.

Read **Lk 22:14-21.**

To conclude this Unit, turn to the **Book of Lamentations** where you will find five poems of sorrow. The poet cries over the destruction of God's Holy City and Temple. You will feel sad and lonely as you picture the ruins of the lovely old city of Jerusalem and realize that God is no longer there living in His Holy Place.

Read **Lam 1.**

a. Read **Mt 23:37.**

b. Were the people of Our Lord's time any different from their ancestors? __________

c. The New Testament speaks of a place of exile far worse than Babylonia. Read **Mt 25:41-46.** Who will go into this place of exile? __________

- Day after day, we hear the prophetic voice of the Church calling us back to God, telling us to confess our sins and accept forgiveness in the sacrament of reconciliation.

A prayer to learn
Lord, we have sinned against you,
Lord have mercy.
Lord, show us your mercy and love,
and grant us your Salvation.

A priest summoning the people to the Feast of Tabernacles

Relief carving, showing the Babylonian Conquest of Palestine

UNIT EIGHT
Exile and after

(An *exile* is a person who is not allowed to live in his own country).

1. To Babylon

Picture a group of prisoners, thin and tired and sad, walking in the hot sun far away to the land of their conquerers. These are God's people going into exile, more than eight hundred kilometres from home. They were already weak when they set out from Jerusalem and many have fallen down on the desert road and died where they fell.

Psalm 137 tells how strange and lonely the exiles felt in Babylon, and in the Book of Lamentations you can find their prayer for mercy.

Read **Ps 137**.

Read **Lam 5**.

- Now we know what has become of God's people . . . and why?
  Can we see ourselves in them?

Look at Map I: *The World of Genesis* (page 25) and take time to study it carefully.

Find: — Canaan (the home of God's people.)
— Egypt, Assyria, & Babylonia (big nations.)
— Syria, Ammon, Moab, & Edom (small nations.)
— The Tigris and Euphrates Rivers
— City of Babylon (notice the distance between Canaan and Babylon.)

2. New problems for the Exiles

Babylonia was a very advanced country. It was large and rich and well-watered by the Tigris and Euphrates Rivers. There were great buildings too and temples bigger and better even that God's Temple in Jerusalem. Each town had its own god and the exiles saw the people taking part in fine processions and ceremonies in honour of their gods. They did not know what to think of all the power and wealth they saw around them. They were amazed; they could not explain why it was that these foreigners were so well off. In their minds, power and wealth were blessings from God. Some of them began to think that the gods of Babylonia must be greater than the God of Israel!

They had another serious problem about worship. Some Eastern peoples thought that you could not worship a god unless you were living in his/her place and since some of the exiles thought like this, they felt it was impossible to worship the God of Israel in Babylonia. Besides they had no temple! Many gave in and followed the Babylonians in worship.

Time passed and some of the exiles settled down and did quite well in Babylonia. They even grew to like this country that seemed to offer more that their own. Some stayed unsettled and spent their time blaming others for all the trouble that had come on them.

But there was a small group who always remembered God's agreement at Mt Sinai: 'You will be my people and I will be your God!' They knew that Babylonia was not the promised land and that they were there because of their sins. They knew that they had shamed the holy God of Israel in the eyes of other nations and that, even though these nations might be proud of themselves, they were still under God and He was 'using' them in His plan of salvation. Furthermore, they held on, *in faith,* to the great promises God had made to their ancestors; they prayed and studied the Law He had given them *through Moses* and they were sure of His love and mercy and power. This is why they were able to believe that there was a great future ahead of them and that God would work wonders for them when the time was right.

This faithful little group learned to look to God more and more and to depend on Him for everything. It is sometimes called 'the poor of Yahweh' because in the Bible 'to be poor' usually means to trust God fully. Sometimes it is called 'the faithful remnant' (remnant = the small piece or few that remain).

God did not forget His 'poor' in their exile. He sent two very great prophets to help them to grow in a spiritual way during the hard years of exile. One of these great prophets was **Ezekiel** (the young priest who had come with them from Jerusalem); the other's name is not known, but people usually call him **the Second Isaiah**.

3. Ezekiel and the Exiles

Ezekiel helped the exiles to realize that God is everywhere and that He can be worshipped in any place. He encouraged them to come together to pray and study the Law of Moses. He had heard the preaching of Jeremiah in Jerusalem and knew that God's presence is not limited to the Temple and that where worship is concerned, the *place* is not nearly as important as the *holiness* of the worshippers.

Ezekiel gave hope and courage to the exiles. In his vision of the dry bones, he saw that God would put an end to the Exile and give Israel a fresh start. He promised that God would bring them home to their own land and take care of them there. He would be their good shepherd.

Hearing the unsettled exiles blaming others for the things that had happened to them, Ezekiel stressed that each person stands before God just as he/she is and that He judges each one separately.

Although this teaching had already been given, it had not been stressed before. Up to this time, the stress had been on the nation before God. This teaching meant that it was no longer possible for a person to hide behind the goodness of others or to pass on blame. On the other hand, God's people could see now that he loved each one separately and gave him/her responsibility. This is so important because it adds dignity to a person. Ezekiel's new stress did not mean that the nation (or group) was any less important in God's eyes. No. In God's plan both the group and the individual has its own privileges and responsibilities and must work them out.

In one of his visions Ezekiel saw the glory of God leaving the Temple in Jerusalem and, in another, he saw the glory of God filling a new Temple. He had planned this new Temple in detail taking care to see that nothing bad would go back into Temple worship. He wanted the new Temple to be kept far away from the palace and he wanted it to have a wide courtyard and a high wall so that the whole space about it could be kept sacred. He saw that great blessings would flow from this sacred Temple of the future.

Read **Ezekiel 3:12-15**: God is everywhere and so Ezekiel went to the exiles.
Ezekiel 36:1-15: God would bring His people home.
Ezekiel 37: God would give new life to Israel.
Ezekiel 34: God would be the good shepherd of His people.
Ezekiel 14:12-23; 18:1-32; 33:10-20: Each person must answer for himself.
Ezekiel 43:1-12: God would return to His sacred Temple.
Ezekiel 47:1-12: Great blessing would flow from the new Temple.

- When the exiles heard the preaching of Ezekiel, they thought of a national restoration; when we hear it, we think of the *final restoration* brought by Jesus.

  In baptism, we receive a new spirit and a heart ready to do God's will. After death, our bodies, like the dry bones, will be raised to life on the Last Day.

  Jesus is the Good Shepherd who brings all people together and leads them home to God in heaven.

  The crucified and risen Body of Jesus is the new Temple from which the lifegiving waters of the Spirit flow.

Read **Ps 40** in a prayerful way, praising and blessing God for the wonder of salvation.

4. Second Isaiah

God wanted Second Isaiah to comfort (or console) His people in exile and to lead them back to Palestine. His work is in the **Book of Isaiah, Chapters 40-55**. In some Bibles these chapters have this heading: *The Book of the Consolation of Israel.* They are written in the same way as the story of the Exodus from Egypt, that is in *epic* style. (Turn back to page 35 and read again what it says about this way of writing.)

This prophet begins by announcing the end of the Exile; the time for going home. His words are full of life and joy and victory.

Read **Isaiah 40:1-31.**

Background: The Babylonian Empire lasted less than a hundred years (612-539 BC). As you know, the Babylonians were rich and they soon fell into a soft and easy way of life. After the death of King Nebuchadnezzar in 562 BC there was no peace in the king's family, only competition and murder. Four kings followed quickly one after the other. The last of the Babylonian kings, Nabonidus was not liked because he honoured the moon god in the city of Babylon, which people believed belonged to the god Marduk. All this made it easy for the Persians to come and take over. *King Cyrus of Persia* was different from other conquerers in that he respected all religions. Sometimes he even practised the religion of the country he conquered! How glad God's people must have been when Cyrus took over! Second Isaiah recognized him as the one God had chosen to allow them to go home.

Read **Isaiah 41:1-5; 45:1-6.**

By his preaching, Second Isaiah made sure that his lesson of the Exile was well known and understood: **There is only one God and He is the Lord and Creator of all things.**

Read **Isaiah 43:8-13; 44:1-20, 24-28.**

Second Isaiah called Israel *the Servant of God.* This is really a beautiful name because it reminds us that Israel belonged to God and that He, like a good master, looked after His servants.

There are four passages (or Songs) describing God's Servant.

The *First Song* tells that the Servant is chosen by God, that His Spirit is with him and that through him the religion of God will be brought to the world in a kind and gentle way.

Read **Isaiah 42:1-4.**

In the *Second Song* the Servant speaks to the nations; he has a message for the whole world.

Read **Isaiah 49:1-6.**

In the *Third Song* the Servant says that his message will bring comfort to many and much sorrow to himself.

Read **Isaiah 50:4-9.**

The *Fourth Song* is the longest. In it God tells how His servant was looked down on by everyone, but in the end raised up for the admiration of all. As you read it, you will surely think of Jesus, our Saviour.

Read **Isaiah 52:13 – 53:12.**

Look up **Mt 12:18-21; Lk 22:37; 1 Pet 2:21b-25.**

Once God's people are home, their sins will be forgotten altogether and they will be taken back into God's love once more.

Read **Isaiah 54:4-10.** Take time to learn by heart one or two verses that you would like to remember.

- The message of Second Isaiah is especially exciting for us because we hear in it the announcement of the coming of Jesus, the Messiah, who will bring in a "new" time when all God's promises will be carried out and the deepest thoughts of His heart made known.

CHANGES IN JUDAISM

We often think of the Exile as a time of spiritual growth and so it was, but there are other important things about it that we must not overlook.

From the time of the Exile onward, the Jerusalem Temple and its ceremonies, the possession of the promised land and kingship *were never again thought of as necessary to religion.*

Another thing too, the Israelites became known as the "Jews" and their religion as *Judaism.* Judaism stressed the importance of:

1. *Studying and reading out the Law of Moses* and
2. *keeping the Sabbath holy.*

This meant that the people needed a place where they could come together, and these meeting places were the beginning of *synagogues.* Later on synagogues were built wherever Jews settled and to the present time synagogues are used as Jewish places of worship. Like all good Jews, our Blessed Lord often went to the synagogue to take part in worship.

Read **Lk 4:16-22.**

5. Apocalyptic Writing

During the Exile many people worked hard on the religious history of Israel and on the laws and practices of their ancestors. Much of their work was written down for future generations. By now, new ways of speaking and writing were beginning to become popular. The strong prophetic preaching that we heard before the Exile, gradually died away and *apocalyptic writing* took its place. This way of writing developed over a long period of time; you have already read some in the **Book of Ezekiel**. The **Book of Daniel** written about 200 BC and the **Book of Revelation** written about 100 AD are apocalyptic writings. The word "apocalyptic" comes from a Greek word that means "to take off a covering that is hiding something". With this kind of writing, men could write about world history in the widest possible way and let all mankind know about an act of God that would bring in "the world to come".

The prophets, as you know, *spoke* to the people of their own times about things that were happening among them. Because God wanted us to benefit from their preaching, He saw to it that their words were not lost. Maybe some of the prophets kept written copies of what they said or perhaps some of their followers wrote it down.

The apocalyptists *wrote* in a symbolic way about "visions" that even they did not fully understand. Angels usually had to be there to explain the meaning of the vision. Apocalyptic writing sounds strange and before you can understand it properly you need to know what the different symbols stand for. Here are just a few examples:

eyes	=	knowledge	the human body
hands	=	power	
legs	=	firmness	
white hair	=	age or majesty	
lion	=	kingship	animals
ox	=	strength	
eagle	=	speed	
dragon	=	evil	
lamb	=	submission	
white	=	joy and victory	colours
red	=	martyrdom	
scarlet	=	wealth	
40	=	perfection	numbers
12	=	the people of God	
1000	=	big crows	

Note: When you are reading apocalyptic writing, you must always remember that the writer is using symbols and that he is pointing ahead to the final victory of God. Some people seem to forget this and so they fill their minds with strange and frightening pictures . . . and miss the message altogether!

Read **Dan 7:1-8. 15-28.**
Read **Rev 1:9-20.**

Some of the psalm writers had the same outlook as the apocalyptic writers. They thought of God as Ruler over all.

Read **Ps 97.**

6. The Return . . . after 70 years

The people of Israel could not believe their ears when they heard King Cyrus' order to return to Jerusalem. They thought they were dreaming! But it was true. God was opening up the way for their return to the land He had promised long ago to Abraham and his descendants.

Read **Ezra 1:2-5**: King Cyrus' order.
Read **Ps 126**: The Song of the returning exiles.

- The song of the returning exiles is one of the most joyful in the whole Bible. This is because the Jews saw clearly that God was doing great things for them. We ought to sing this song with even deeper joy because in setting us free from sin, God has done much greater things for us. When our turn comes to leave this world of exile behind, we can go with confidence to our true home in heaven, where we will live forever in the light and peace of God's presence.

The exiles did not go home alone. God was with them and once more His glory shone on the city of Jerusalem. It became again what He had always wanted it to be . . . "a light to the nations".

Read **Isaiah 60:1-22.**

- The Church takes a passage from this lovely chapter for the Feast of the Epiphany and applies it to herself. The presence of Christ in His Church and the truth of her teaching makes her *the gathering place for all nations.*

7. Starting again

As you would expect, not all the Jews returned to Jerusalem. Some preferred to stay where they were. After all, most of them had never seen Palestine; they had only heard about it from their parents or grandparents. (The Exile lasted about fifty years.) Those who chose to go home, formed into groups and left when they felt they were ready. The first group set out in 537 or 536 BC. One of the main groups was led by *Zerubbabel* who had been made governor of Judah by the Persians. He was a High Priest as well.

Zerubbabel was most probably the man who started the work of re-building the Temple. The Jews had been back in Palestine less than two years when this important work was begun. They must have had a hard time in the beginning trying to get land and grow food and organize their community.

Some people did not welcome them either and the Samaritans were a real nuisance to them. (The Assyrians had settled these people in the Northern Kingdom after the fall of Samaria in 721 BC.)

The Samaritans interfered so much with the building of the Temple that the work had to stop. After fifteen years, it was the Prophet Haggai who stirred the people to get on with the work again. As far as he could see, the Samaritans were not the only ones to blame for the long delay. The Jews themselves had weak faith and no real interest in this holy work.

Read **Haggai 1:2-15.**

After five years the Temple was finished . . . and some people were disappointed with it! They felt that it was a poor type of building (perhaps they remembered the great temples in Babylon) and certainly not to be compared with Solomon's Temple. Haggai encouraged these people. The building itself was not so important; they should try to think more about what it stood for. He said they should *look ahead* not back, because God had great plans for *this* Temple of theirs and for the future. In fact, He was already rewarding them for their faith and goodwill.

Read **Haggai 2:1-9. 15-19.**

8. A new "age"

Zechariah was another prophet who advised the people *to look to the future.* There was no sense in sorrowing over the past; that was done with and a time of peace and happiness was coming when God would stay with them forever.

Read **Zechariah 8:1-23; 9:1-17; 10:1-12.**

There were other prophets in this period, some whose names we do not know, who gave this same message: Look to the future, a 'new' time is coming, a new 'age'. It will be an 'age' of peace and glory and there will be so much of everything that everyone will have more than he needs.

Read: **Malachi 4:1-5**: An unknown prophet. Malachi means 'my messenger'.
Joel 2:18-32
Isaiah 61:1 – 63:14: An unknown prophet who is often called *Third Isaiah.*

Worldly-minded people thought that these prophets were saying that God was going to make Judah great and powerful and free again as in the days of King David and give them a perfect king, a descendant of the royal house of David. But when men and women of faith, like 'the poor of Yahweh', thought about all that had gone before, they realized that these prophets were speaking about something spiritual. Besides, their faith in the power and will of God *to save* had grown so much that they were able to think of higher things . . . They did not set their hearts on an earthly kingdom, but on the reign of God over all mankind in a Kingdom "not of this world".

It was the people of the New Testament times who experienced the coming of the new 'age'. They knew that, in Jesus, God is present in the world exercising His kingship.

- From the parables of Jesus we know a great deal about the Kingdom of God, but still it is a mystery and we must go on wondering and waiting for it to come in all its fullness.

  a. Here are a few New Testament passages that you might like to read . . . there are many others about the *Kingdom of God.*
  Mk 1:15; Lk 13:18-21; Lk 17:20-21; Mt 5:3-10.

  b. The New Testament people found in Jesus *the perfect king* who was both Son of David and Son of God. Read **Mt 21:1-10; Jn 18:36-38.**

9. Ezra and Nehemiah

About seventy years after the Temple was finished two very great men appeared in the Jewish community in Jerusalem. They are **Ezra** and **Nehemiah** and probably both had come from the Persian court.

Nehemiah's main work was to organize the building of a wall around Jerusalem. This wall was necessary for protection against enemies and it also marked Jerusalem off as a place with a religion of its own. This was a safeguard against false religions.

Nehemiah was trusted by the King of Persia and had his support against the Samaritans who wanted to stop the building of the wall, just as they had stopped the building of the Temple years before. Nehemiah was made Governor of Judah by the Persians and this meant that Jerusalem was now free of Samaritan control.

Read **Nehemiah 2:1-20**: Nehemiah goes to Jerusalem
4:1-23: The Samaritans tried to stop Nehemiah's work.
12:27-43: The walls were dedicated to God.

Ezra was not concerned with building a wall or a temple. He wanted to build up the religion that these stood for. As a priest, his chief concern was *worship.* His aim was to see that worship was carried out with reverence and to prepare the people for worship by bringing their lives into line with the Law of God. Ezra had made a special study of the Law; he saw that many Jews had grown careless in religion and were in great danger of being drawn away again to the worship of foreign gods.

Read **Ezra**: **7:1-28**: Ezra arrives in Jerusalem.
8:15-30: Ezra is concerned about worship.
9:1 – 10:17: The people were not living by the Law of God.

The settling of the marriages was a very serious matter and you might wonder about it. Did you notice that the Jews *themselves* said that they had done wrong? They knew that in marrying foreigners, they were doing harm to their religion. (Do you remember why King Solomon ended badly?) Ezra wanted the Jews to separate themselves from foreigners for the sake of their religion. How could they hope to worship God properly and keep their community together if they were not firmly attached to God and clear about their duties. Once they had made up their minds again to be faithful to Him, Ezra led them into a closer relationship with Him through a solemn covenant.

Read **Nehemiah 9:1-38; 10:28-29.**

Note: It is thanks to Ezra that *Judaism* (explained on p.87) developed in the right way in the years following the Exile. Moved by the example of Ezra, many men began to study the Law closely and to explain it to the people. (These men were called *Scribes.*) The Law that God has given through Moses had always been important in the life of God's People, but in this period, it became the very centre of their lives. Not only their religion, but their whole way of life was organized around it and to keep the Law was the mark of a Jew.

10. Religious writing after the Exile

Very much *religious writing* was done after the Exile. You have read passages from some of the prophets of the Restoration: Haggai; Zechariah; Malachi; Joel. An outstanding writer of this period is known as **the Chronicler.** His four books are **1 and 2 Chronicles; Ezra; Nehemiah.**

The passages that you read from the **Books of Ezra** and **Nehemiah,** show that the Chronicler had a special interest in worship and in the Law. **1 and 2 Chronicles,** taken together, form a kind of history of Israel written to show the Jews that God's chosen people had not been wiped out during the Exile. Far from it! This small Jewish community that was trying to organize itself around the Law was linked to the kingdom of David and was, therefore, God's own community . . . *and ought to be a holy community.* You might think that the Chronicler has just repeated many of the things that we already know about Israel's history from the Pentateuch and from the Books of Samuel and Kings, and that is so, but the importance of his work lies in the way he explained their meaning.

In his history of Israel, the Chronicler paid special attention to the Promise made to King David and to the good things done for religion by kings of David's royal line. In doing this, *he stirred up fresh hope for the fulfillment of God's Promise to David.* The time seemed very close now for the coming of the Messiah and the perfect Kingdom of God.

The Book of Jonah was probably written about the time Ezra was directing the Jewish community. In a half-serious, half-entertaining way, the author tells his Jewish readers: Yes; you are very important; you are God's chosen people, but don't forget that you are not the only people God made. There are plenty of others besides youselves and God loves them too and for good reasons.

If you like, you can stop here to read the **Book of Jonah,** or leave it till later. It is very enjoyable and not long either, but be careful afterwards not to lose the thread of *the story* of God's people that we have been following since the call of Abraham.

BACKGROUND TO THE RELIGIOUS HISTORY OF THE JEWS

The Persian Empire came to an end in 331 BC. It was a young Greek called Alexander the Great, with his fine soldiers, who defeated the Persians and set up the Greek empire. His idea was to unite all the peoples of his empire into one. He thought this could be done by spreading the Greek language and culture. He built new cities in different places modelled on the Greek style. The city of Alexandria in Egypt was one of these and it is important to us because it was there that the *Greek Bible* was produced.

After his death, Alexander's empire split into two parts and even though the leaders fought for control of Palestine, the Jews were left free to practise their religion and to run their lives in the way that suited them. But the world about them was changing! Cities in the Greek style were being built in Palestine and the Greek way of life was spreading there. The Greeks had good schools and sports-grounds and theatres and many of the Jews were strongly attracted by these and by the ideas they learned in them. Many would gladly have done away with their 'old' way of life. Others were just the opposite! When they realized how popular Greek things were becoming, they clung more strongly than ever to the Law and to all their Jewish practices. So the Jewish community was split over this matter of 'going Greek'.

Things were made worse by political troubles that came about because some rulers (High Priests) of the Jewish community were ready to pay bribes and make promises to the Greeks and some Jews fought among themselves for the position of High Priest.

Note: After the Exile, the *High Priest* was the most important person in the Jewish community. He led the people in worship; he was head of the ruling group called the Council (or Sanhedrin) and he was spokesman for the Jews with their foreign rulers. Like kings in the time before the Exile, he was 'anointed' and was therefore a sacred person, even though he might be very unworthy in himself. Caiaphas, who was High Priest in the time of Jesus, was one of this type. He was the first to say that Jesus should be put to death and the plans for the arrest of Jesus were made in his house. He was the one, also, who asked the question that enabled the court to sentence Jesus to death.

Look up: **Jn 11:49-52; Mt 26:3-5; Mt 26:62-67.**

The following references tell of division among the Jews in Palestine and how those Jews who refused to 'go Greek' suffered and died. (You will not be able to follow this period unless 1 and 2 Maccabees are in your Bible.)

Read **2 Maccabees 4:7-37; 5:11-23**: Bad leaders; evil deeds.
6:1-11; 6:18-23; 7:1-42: Suffering; death.

A group of brave and fervent Jews organized themselves around their leader Judas Maccabeus and fought for religious freedom. They were successful, but their people did not enjoy their success for long. Jewish leaders became caught up again in political matters and Palestine was open to attack once more. This time it was the Romans. They took over in 63 BC and, when New Testament times began, the proud and cruel *Herod the Great* was acting as King of Judea. It was at this very unlikely time in history that Israel's *Prophet-King* arrived . . . the One for whom 'the poor of Yahweh' has been waiting.

See how the New Testament writers describe this amazing event.

Read **Mt 1:18-25; Lk 1:1-38; Lk 2:1-20.**

- Throughout the interesting history of the chosen people, the living and true God made Himself *known upon the earth.* The Almighty God of Israel, a teacher without equal, took almost two thousand years to build up the faith of His people and to lift their hopes to a high spiritual level. When "the fullness of time came", His faithful ones were ready to receive the Messiah and his message about the Kingdom of God.

A prayer to learn:

Father, you so loved the world
that in the fullness of time you sent your only Son to be our Saviour.
He was conceived through the power of the Holy Spirit,

and born of the Virgin Mary,
a man like us in all things but sin.
To the poor he proclaimed the good news of salvation,
to the prisoner, freedom,
and to those in sorrow, joy.

(Eucharistic Prayer 4)

List of important dates in salvation history

It is not possible to give exact dates for the events in salvation history, especially for the earlier years down to the death of Solomon in 931 BC. From this time, dating is more exact, but still might not be quite right.

Note: c. = about. All these date are *Before Christ* (BC)

c. 1800 – *c.* 1600	Time of the Patriarchs.
c. 1600 – *c.* 1250	Israelites in Egypt.
c. 1250	The Exodus.
c. 1250 – *c.* 1210	The wandering in the Desert.
c. 1210 – *c.* 1030	Conquest and Settlement in Canaan.
c. 1030 – *c.* 1010	The reign of King Saul.
c. 1010 – *c.* 970	The reign of King David.
c. 970 – *c.* 931	The reign of Solomon.
931 –	The Division of the Kingdom: Israel & Judah.
722	The Fall of the Northern Kingdom (Samaria).
587	The Fall of the Southern Kingdom (Jerusalem).
587 – 538	The Exile.
538	King Cyrus allows the Jews to Return.
537	Foundation of the New Temple.
445 – 443	Rebuilding of the Walls of Jerusalem.
331	The Greek Empire is set up.
166 – 63	The Jews have Independence.
63 –	The Romans arrive in Palestine.
37 – 4	Herod the Great ruled Judea.

Supplement

In this course, we have followed the main events in salvation history and tried to see the religious message in them for the people of Israel and for ourselves.

Now I would like to draw your attention to some remarkable stories that God has given us through human authors to add to our knowledge of Himself and to build up our faith and true religious attitudes to life.

The Book of Job: In this Book, the author looks at the problem of suffering and tries to discover why God allows an innocent man to suffer. This book was probably written during the Exile or shortly after it. It is written in a beautiful poetic style and the answer to the problem is worked out in the form of a discussion between Job and his friends.

The Book of Tobit: The author of the Book of Tobit has given his readers a fine story to teach them that goodness is rewarded and that life is worth living. This book teaches us very much about family virtues.

The Book of Esther: The message of the Book of Esther is that God does not forget His people, but always comes to help them in time of trouble. The writer has given a Persian background to his story, but it is almost certain that the Persian empire was finished when this story was written.

The Book of Judith: The prayer of Judith in Chapter 9 is the key to this Book. Because of her firm trust, God could act through her for the salvation of His people. It is thought that this Book was written to encourage the Jews when they were being persecuted in the second century BC.

The Book of Daniel: The author of the Book of Daniel had a deep dislike for the ways of the Greeks and a strong devotion to the Law of God. Through his story, he tried to build up the faith of the Jews and strengthen them when they were suffering under the Greeks. His work is presented in an apocalyptic style of writing.

The Book of Jonah: The Book of Jonah is listed among the prophetical books, though it is quite different from them. In the *story,* Jonah is presented as a true prophet to whom God has entrusted a message . . . not for the Chosen People, but for foreigners! See p.92.